Food in the City

Food in the City

in the

LOVE FOOD

First published in 2009
Love Food ® is an imprint of Parragon Books Ltd

Parragon
Queen Street House
4 Queen Street
Bath BA1 1HE, UK

Copyright © Parragon Books Ltd 2009

Love Food ® and the accompanying heart device is a trademark of Parragon Books Ltd

ISBN: 978-1-4075-6436-4

Printed in Malaysia

Project managed by Faye Lloyd
Written by Beverly Le Blanc
Foreword by Clodagh McKenna
Designed by Andrew Easton @ Ummagumma
Photography by Mike Cooper
Food styling by Lincoln Jefferson

PICTURE ACKNOWLEDGEMENTS
The publisher would like to thank the following for permission to reproduce copyright material:

Getty images pages 8, 9, 10, 11, 12–13, 18–19, 26–27, 32–33, 36–37, 44, 52–53, 54–55, 60–61, 68–69, 74–75, 78–79, 85, 86, 94–95, 96–97, 102–103, 116–117, 120–121, 127, 128, 136–137, 138–139, 144–145, 152–153, 158–159, 162–163, 169, 170, 178–179, 180–181, 186–187, 194–195, 199–200, 204–205

iStockphoto images pages 4, 5, 14, 16, 20, 24, 28–29, 34, 38, 40, 42, 46, 48, 49, 50, 64, 72, 76, 82, 100–101, 108, 110–111, 122, 124, 132, 133, 134, 140, 142, 143, 148–149, 156, 202, 212, 218, 220, 221

Notes for the Reader

This book uses imperial, metric, and US cup measurements. Follow the same units of measurement throughout; do not mix imperial and metric. All spoon measurements are level: teaspoons are assumed to be 5 ml, and tablespoons are assumed to be 15 ml. Unless otherwise stated, milk is assumed to be whole, eggs and individual vegetables, such as potatoes, are medium, and pepper is freshly ground black pepper.

The times given are an approximate guide only. Preparation times differ according to the techniques used by different people and the cooking times may also vary from those given as a result of the type of oven used. Optional ingredients, variations, or serving suggestions have not been included in the calculations.

Recipes using raw or very lightly cooked eggs should be avoided by infants, the elderly, pregnant women, convalescents, and anyone with a chronic condition. Pregnant and breast-feeding women are advised to avoid eating peanuts and peanut products. People with nut allergies should be aware that some of the prepared ingredients used in the recipes in this book may contain nuts. Always check the packaging before use.

CONTENTS:

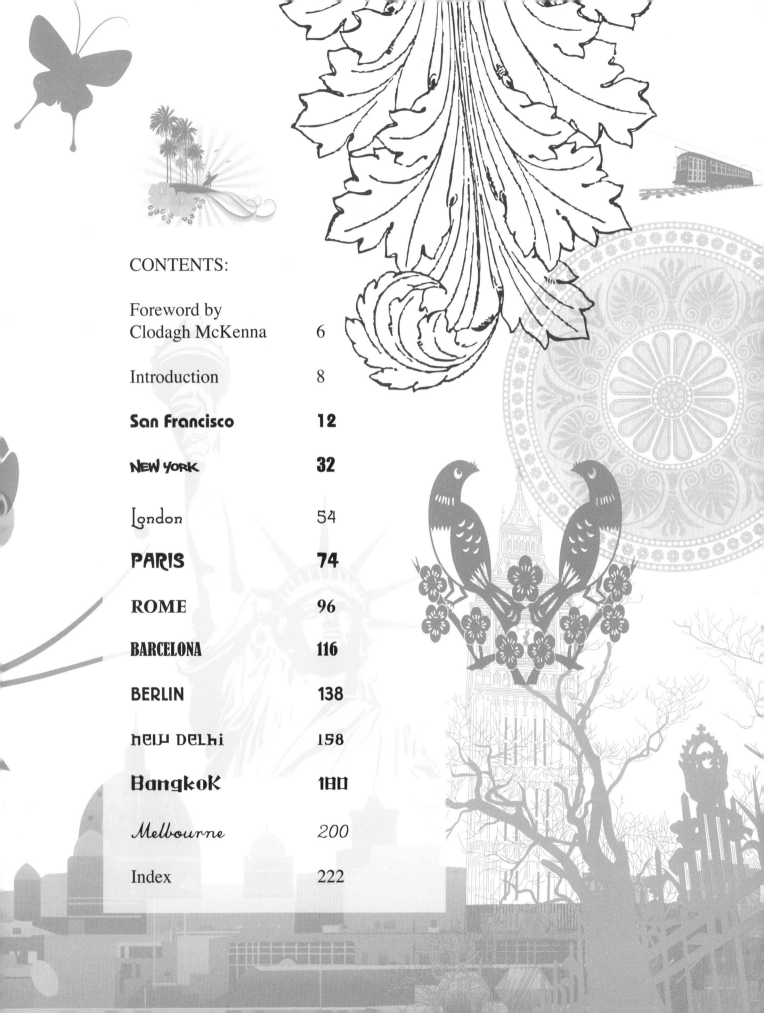

Foreword

My passion for food has taken me around the world. I studied in Paris and New York; I trained and worked as a chef at Ballymaloe in West Cork in Ireland; I live in Turin, Italy, and my work takes me to the United States, England and Ireland. One of the great joys of so much moving around is getting to dine out in different cities. For me, a city is defined by food; I remember places by taste. When I arrive I seek out the markets. I want to eat where the locals eat and I have to sample the city's signature dish to really get the essence of a place. When I leave all I can think about is getting back to my own kitchen and re-creating the dishes!

You can tell a lot about the character of a city by its restaurants and cafés. In Melbourne the cafés on every corner, buzzing with students and business people, and the exquisite fish restaurants on the sea front equally reflect the confidence and cosmopolitan mix of this sunny city. In London, you can bolster yourself with organ meat dishes in fashionable restaurants, using recipes that go back hundreds of years. Here, the sense of history is as evident in the food as it is in the walls of the Tower of London.

A city's food gives us a snapshot of its history. When in New York, I'm always struck by how each wave of immigrants has stamped its identity on the city's cuisine, which is apparent in Chinatown, Little Italy, the Irish bars, and Jewish delis. In Italy, each region is fiercely proud of its local produce and the dish that defines it. The local dish defines people's identity as much as dialect or traditional costume.

Food, almost more than photos can evoke a sense of time and place, bringing back memories of where the dish was originally eaten. When I think of Paris, I think of being a student, tucking into sumptuous Croque Monsieur at small cafés along the Seine.

For me, Naples will always be about the best pizza I ever ate; the base was thin and crisp and the topping so fresh and the taste so vivid that my taste buds are still in mourning for the last mouthful. Serving tapas always transports me back to the bars in Barcelona; standing with individual dishes of chorizo, anchovies, and tortilla, drinking a glass of cold beer, and watching the world go by.

The food of each city and how they eat it tells us how the citizens structure their time, and mark the celebrations and rituals of their lives. It is sensual and social—a way of preserving tradition and a wonderful way of getting to know and celebrating each other's cultures.

—Clodagh McKenna,
Chef and international food writer

Introduction

This book is a celebration of the best regional food from around the world. It lets you sample the tastes and traditions of what are arguably the top ten culinary cities where food culture is a significant part of the urban mix that makes each area unique.

Unlike country food, traditionally meant to fuel hard physical work and stretch ingredients to feed large numbers, city food gives cooks more scope for innovation and experimentation, updating favorite recipes and making the most of new and unusual local ingredients. As young chefs flock to cities, they bring with them an enthusiasm and a new approach that soon influences other professional and domestic cooks. And, of course, the multiculturalism of cities—especially New York, San Francisco, London, and Melbourne.

The influence of city food, ultimately affecting what we all eat and cook, is illustrated by reflecting on nouvelle cuisine, the French cooking style that put great emphasis on preparing and cooking fresh ingredients in a lighter style with stunning presentation. It swept through Paris kitchens in the 1960s and 1970s, eventually being adopted by chefs around the world, and finally reinventing itself as New American Cuisine in the San Francisco area in the 1980s. The emphasis placed by chefs there on using locally sourced, seasonal ingredients as they adapted nouvelle cuisine for American palates helped expand farmers' markets throughout the country, a legacy that continues. As the new-wave cooking style crossed the Pacific, Melbourne chefs were at the forefront, shaking up Australia's food culture to produce what is known as Mod Oz food, injecting a breath of fresh air into the contemporary cooking scene. Now the movement has gone full cycle, as young Australian chefs bring their idea of fusion cooking to European kitchens and beyond.

The joy of preparing city food is the never ending variety. Even in these days of globalization, the food from each of these cities is unique. Cooks in San Francisco and New York City might be American, but it isn't difficult to identify which recipes come from which coast, making the cooks more like distant cousins than sisters and brothers. In Europe, food from Barcelona, Berlin, London, Paris, and Rome looks different, tastes different, and has evolved out of different traditions, even though they are all major metropolises. Traveling eastward, cooks in New Delhi, Bangkok, and Melbourne borrow from each other and use similar flavorings but still produce uniquely different styles of food.

City food also offers exciting dining experiences. Restaurant meals can be sophisticated and upmarket, or inexpensive and casual. Paris is renowned worldwide for its fine restaurants with their glittering Michelin stars, but all the other cities in this book also offer opportunities for fine dining. And cities as diverse as New York, New Delhi, and Bangkok share the tradition of food-on-the-go, be it well-packed sandwiches or street food cooked to order at tiny roadside stalls.

A Culinary Cornucopia

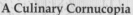
The recipes in this book highlight the quintessential flavors and cooking style of each city. In the United States, for example, New York and San Francisco dominate the food culture of both coasts, but each has its own culinary personality. Both cities have their own way of reflecting the tastes of home brought by the waves of European immigrants in the nineteenth and twentieth centuries. New York became the country's melting pot, but it is the impact of the Eastern Europeans that stands out on menus today in the form of Potato Knishes, Reuben Sandwiches, Bagels, and New York Cheesecake. On the Pacific coast, large numbers of Italian dockworkers have left their mark with Cioppino, the American version of Mediterranean seafood stews, and food of various Asian communities, especially the Chinese, is readily available. Stopping to enjoy dim sum is a popular San Francisco pastime.

Many European cooks, however, tend to remain more loyal to established traditions, giving modern twists to old favorites. Two notable exceptions, however, occur in Paris, where couscous restaurants are a direct import from former foreign colonies, and London. Modern London is such a multicultural mix that food from most global cuisines is served alongside British favorites, such as Bubble & Squeak, Roast Pork Belly, and Spotted Dick with Custard. There has been a seismic change in the variety and quality of food readily available in the past decade as "pub grub" has been elevated to restaurant standard and TV chefs achieve celebrity status.

Cooks in Berlin cater for hearty appetites with large portions and often devise menus to be enjoyed with a stein of local beer. However, Germans are becoming aware of the need for healthier eating habits, so it is now possible to enjoy lighter meals, although vegetarians can have a difficult time finding much choice as pork remains king. The city also offers Turkish, Middle Eastern, and Indian choices. In Rome, cooks are guided by the seasons in an almost religious way. Even something as simple as preparing a plate of pasta is guided by the calendar—in summer, it will be tossed with chunks of fresh tomato and mozzarella cheese, or served with the lightest imaginable sauce of lemon and tuna; in winter, it is more likely to be dressed with oil and garlic, or a black olive sauce.

The tapas culture of Barcelona is one of the city's defining characteristics. For visitors to the city, hopping from tapas bar to tapas bar is an enjoyable way to replace a set meal, but for the locals it just takes the edge off their hunger before their late-hour evening meal. Baby Fava Beans & Chorizo and Tomato-Rubbed Bread are traditional, but modern ideas include Fideuà, similar to the well-known paella, but made with thin noodles instead of rice.

Dining experiences in New Delhi mirror the city's extremes—they can be sublime and sophisticated, or very basic and rough at a subsistence level. You'll find both Hindu and Muslim food with plenty of dishes that reflect the once great Mughal legacy. For an adventure, go to bustling Chandni Chowk, in Old Delhi, where stalls cooking pakoras, parathas, and all types of street food sit alongside those selling jewelry, saris, and just about anything else anyone could want.

Street food is also a significant part of the Bangkok dining experience. It is said wherever you are in the city you are never more than 55 yards/50 meters from a restaurant or food stall. This gives you a chance to sample all of Thailand's regional specialties, as well as food from China, India, the rest of Asia, and many western countries. The other joy for visitors is that you aren't restricted by conventional mealtimes—you can eat around the clock in Bangkok. If time permits, schedule a stop at the numerous open-air markets *(tàlàats)* to view the dazzling array of produce. Floating markets *(tàlàat náat am)* along the canals were once a regular sight, but now, alas, only one exists, at Bang Sai, more to satisfy tourist curiosity than local needs. Or take a bus to Damnoen Saduak, about 50 miles/80 kilometers southwest of the capital, to see the largest floating market.

Melbourne is a city that takes its laid-back attitudes to food very seriously. You'll find a choice of eateries wherever you are—from the popular Italian-inspired cafés to Mod Oz, traditional and heritage restaurants, and endless foreign restaurants—with the St. Kilda area offering a bit of everything. The cultural mix of the population inspires plenty of ethnic restaurants and food markets, with Mediterranean, North African, Greek, and Asian cuisines available.

Basically, city food, wherever you are in the world, has something for everyone. To paraphrase English writer Samuel Johnson (1709–84), when a man is tired of city food, he is tired of eating.

San Francisco

Freshness is the hallmark of cooking in San Francisco. Blessed with a temperate climate and the teeming Pacific, the Bay Area's cooks have an abundance of fruit, vegetables, and seafood to choose from, along with splendid wines from nearby vineyards. Consequently, perhaps it's no surprise the American farmers' market movement took hold here. And when the large Asian and Mexican populations add their flavorings to indigenous ingredients, San Francisco food takes on a distinctive style. Yet, even with so much choice, the sweet meat of the Dungeness crab remains unsurpassed in popularity. Although it is fished all along the California coast, local cooks have adopted it, and natives and tourists alike flock to Fisherman's Wharf to sample it in traditional dishes, such as Cioppino, a hearty seafood stew.

Dim Sum

Method

To make the wrappers, put the flour in a bowl, making a well in the middle. Slowly pour in the water, mixing with a wooden spoon until a rough dough forms. Add extra flour, if necessary, to absorb all the water. When cool enough to handle, shape into a soft ball and turn out onto a lightly floured counter. Knead for 5 minutes, or until smooth and elastic. Shape the dough into a ball, cover, and let rest for 30 minutes.

Meanwhile, put all the filling ingredients into a bowl with pepper to taste and use your hands to squeeze together until blended. Set aside. Mix all the ingredients for the dipping sauce together and set aside.

Divide the dough into 14 equal-size balls and cover those you aren't working with with a clean cloth. Flatten the balls between your palms, then roll them out into circles about 4 inches/10 cm across. Use a 3¼-inch/8-cm cutter to cut out circles. Place a teaspoon of filling in each circle and fold the dough to make half-moon shapes, pressing to seal the edges.

Heat a large wok with a tight-fitting lid over a high heat. Add a very thin layer of oil and heat. Add the dumplings, flat side down, and fry for 2–3 minutes, moving occasionally to prevent sticking, until golden brown on the bottoms. Do not overcrowd the wok. Pour in the stock, immediately cover the wok, and let steam for 5 minutes, or until all the liquid has evaporated. Remove one dumpling from the wok and cut in half to check that the filling is cooked through. Serve at once with the soy sauce dipping sauce.

Ingredients

Makes 14

3¼ oz/90 g ground pork

3¼ oz/90 g cooked, shelled shrimp, minced

1½-inch/4-cm piece of carrot, peeled and grated

2 scallions, white parts only, very finely chopped

1 large garlic clove, crushed

1½ tbsp cornstarch

1 tsp grated fresh ginger

2 tsp soy sauce

2 tsp rice vinegar

2 tsp sesame oil

1 tsp hoisin sauce

black pepper

sunflower oil or peanut oil, for frying

⅔ cup chicken stock or vegetable stock, for steaming

soy sauce, for dipping

WRAPPERS

about 1 cup all-purpose flour, plus extra for dusting

½ cup boiling water

Beet, Fennel & avocado salad with ricotta salata

Ingredients

Serves 4–6

2 avocados, halved, pitted, and thinly sliced

2 fennel bulbs, trimmed and thinly sliced

2 golden, striped, or ruby cooked beets, peeled and thinly sliced

2 tbsp snipped chives

2 tbsp finely chopped fresh parsley

1 tbsp finely shredded fresh basil

1 tbsp finely chopped fresh mint

⅓ cup grated ricotta salata cheese

DRESSING

½ cup sunflower oil

2 tbsp fresh orange juice

salt and pepper

Method

To make the dressing, put the oil and orange juice in a large, nonmetallic bowl and whisk until blended. Add salt and pepper to taste.

Add the avocado and fennel to the bowl and toss with your hands to coat in the dressing. (At this point the salad can be covered with plastic wrap and chilled for up to 4 hours.)

When ready to serve, arrange the beet slices on a serving platter or individual plates. Add the herbs to the bowl with the fennel and avocado and toss together. Stir the cheese into the bowl and toss again, then mound the salad on top of the beet slices.

Cioppino with focaccia toast

Ingredients

Serves 4–6

2 tbsp butter

2 tbsp olive oil

3 large garlic cloves, crushed

2 green bell peppers, cored, seeded, and chopped

2 large onions, chopped

large pinch saffron threads

14 oz/400 g canned crushed tomatoes

1 cup dry red wine

2 tbsp tomato paste

3 tbsp lemon juice, plus extra to taste

1 bay leaf

1 tsp fennel seeds

pinch of sugar

Tabasco sauce, to taste

14 oz/400 g clams, scrubbed

14 oz/400 g mussels scrubbed and beards removed

1lb/450 g boneless white fish, such as sea bass, cut into large chunks

9 oz/250 g shelled scallops

14 oz/400 g shrimp, shelled and deveined

2 cooked Dungeness crabs, dressed, and cracked into pieces

salt and pepper

8–12 slices rosemary focaccia, toasted and brushed with olive oil, to serve

Method

Melt the butter with the oil in a large lidded casserole over medium heat. Add the garlic, bell peppers, and onions and fry for 5 minutes, stirring.

Add the saffron, tomatoes, wine, tomato paste, lemon juice, bay leaf, fennel seeds, sugar, and Tabasco sauce and salt and pepper to taste. Bring to a boil, stirring, then reduce the heat to very low, cover, and simmer for 1 hour. Adjust the seasoning, adding lemon juice, Tabasco sauce, and salt and pepper to taste.

Discard any open clams and mussels that do not close when tapped. Add the seafood to the broth in the order it needs to be cooked: clams and mussels, 5 minutes; sea bass, 4–6 minutes; scallops and shrimp, 1–2 minutes; and cooked crab just long enough to warm through.

Discard any unopened clams and mussels and the crab shells. Ladle the cioppino into bowls and serve with the focaccia.

Heirloom tomato & artichoke frittata

Method

Heat 2 tablespoons of oil in a 10-inch/25-cm skillet over medium heat. Add the leek and stir for 2 minutes. Add the tomatoes and stir for an additional 2 minutes. Transfer the vegetables to the eggs using a slotted spoon, then add the artichokes, parsley, cheese, and salt and pepper to taste. Scrape off any sediment stuck to the bottom of the skillet.

Reheat the skillet over high heat until a splash of water "dances" on the surface. Add 1 tablespoon of oil to the skillet, swirling to coat the side. Pour in the egg mixture and cook gently for 5–6 minutes, or until the underside is just set and lightly browned. Use a spatula to loosen the frittata away from the side and bottom of the pan to let the uncooked egg run underneath and prevent the frittata from sticking to the bottom.

Remove the pan from the heat, cover the frittata with a large, upside-down plate, and invert the frittata onto it. Slide the frittata back into the pan, cooked-side up, and cook for another 2–3 minutes, until the underside is lightly browned.

Let stand for 2 minutes, then slide the frittata onto a serving plate. Serve warm or at room temperature, cut into wedges.

Ingredients

Serves 4

3–4 tbsp canola oil, olive oil, or sunflower oil

1 leek, halved lengthwise, thinly sliced, and rinsed

2 firm red and/or yellow heirloom tomatoes, peeled, seeded, and chopped

8 extra-large eggs, beaten in a large bowl

4 artichoke hearts in oil, drained and quartered lengthwise

2 tbsp chopped fresh parsley

2 tbsp freshly grated Parmesan cheese

salt and pepper

Crab risotto with lemon & parsley

Ingredients

Serves 4

2 tbsp butter

2 tbsp mild-flavored olive oil

1 fennel bulb, trimmed and finely chopped

1½ cups arborio or other short-grain risotto rice

4 tbsp dry white Vermouth or dry white wine

about 1¼ cups fish stock, simmering

1 lb/450 g lump crab leg meat

finely grated zest of 2 large lemons

4 tbsp chopped fresh parsley

pinch of cayenne pepper (optional)

salt and pepper

Method

Melt the butter with the oil in a heavy-bottom saucepan over medium–high heat. Add the fennel and stir for 5 minutes, or until softened.

Stir in the rice so all the grains are coated in oil. Add the Vermouth, stirring until it evaporates.

Add a ladleful of the hot stock and stir until it is absorbed. Continue adding the stock, ladleful by ladleful, stirring continuously, for 20 minutes.

Stir in the crab, half the lemon zest, and half the parsley, then continue adding the stock until the crab is cooked through and the grains are tender but with a slight bite and the risotto is creamy. (You might not need to use all the stock.) Be careful not to break up all the chunky pieces of crabmeat.

Stir in the cayenne pepper, if using, and add salt and pepper to taste. Stir in the remaining lemon zest and parsley. Spoon into warmed bowls and serve.

Red wine-braised beef short ribs

Ingredients

Serves 4–6

about 5 tbsp canola oil or sunflower oil

4 lb 8 oz/2 kg bone-in beef short ribs, cut into 4-inch/10-cm pieces

1 large onion, chopped

1 large carrot, peeled and chopped

1 celery stalk, chopped

1 bottle dry red wine, such as California Zinfandel

4½ cups beef stock

1 bouquet garni of parsley, thyme, and a bay leaf

4 tbsp butter

1 lb 9 oz/700 g portobello mushrooms, wiped and thickly sliced

1 tbsp fresh thyme leaves, or ½ tbsp dried thyme leaves

salt and pepper

chopped fresh parsley, to garnish

Method

Preheat the oven to 325°F/160°C. Heat 4 tablespoons of oil in a large casserole over medium–high heat. Brown the ribs on all sides in batches, adding more oil if necessary, and set aside. Add the onion, carrot, and celery and fry for 5 minutes until tender. Spoon off any excess fat. Pour in the wine and stock, and bring to a boil.

Reduce the heat and return the ribs to the casserole with the bouquet garni, salt and pepper to taste, and enough water to cover. Scrunch a piece of foil on top, cover, and return to a boil. Put in the preheated oven for 1½ hours, or until the ribs are just tender. Do not overcook.

Skim the copious amount of fat from the surface, remove the ribs, and strain the liquid. Return the ribs and liquid to the casserole and set aside.

Melt the butter with 1 tablespoon of the oil in a large skillet. Add the mushrooms and stir for 2 minutes. Add the thyme and salt and pepper to taste, then stir for an additional 3 minutes, or until the mushrooms give off their liquid.

Stir the mushrooms into the casserole. Place over a medium–high heat and let bubble slightly, uncovered, for 45 minutes, until the sauce is reduced and thick. Remove any loose bones. Adjust the seasoning, sprinkle with parsley, and serve.

Slow-roasted duck legs

Ingredients

Serves 4

4 duck legs

2 lb 4 oz/1 kg turnips, peeled and cut into large chunks

2 tbsp butter

2 tbsp sunflower oil

½ cup chicken stock or vegetable stock

1½ tbsp light brown sugar

2 lb/900 g curly kale, thick central stems removed, chopped, and well rinsed

salt and pepper

chopped fresh parsley, to garnish

Method

Preheat the oven to 300°F/150°C. Heat a large ovenproof skillet over high heat. Season the duck legs with salt and pepper, put in the skillet, skin-side down, and fry for 3–5 minutes, until browned. Cover the skillet with foil and transfer to the preheated oven for 90 minutes, basting once or twice with the rendered fat, or until the meat is tender.

After 60 minutes of the duck cooking time, prepare the turnips. Bring a saucepan of lightly salted water to a boil, add the turnips, and cook for 3–5 minutes. Drain and pat dry. Melt the butter with the oil in a large skillet over medium–high heat. Add the turnips and fry, turning frequently, for 5–8 minutes, until brown on all sides. Add the stock and sugar and bring to a boil, stirring gently for 10 minutes, or until the liquid reduces to a glaze and the turnips are tender. Season with salt and pepper, sprinkle with parsley, and keep warm.

Meanwhile, put the curly kale in a large saucepan of water, bring to a boil, and drain. Return to the pan with fresh water, bring to a boil, and cook for 5–7 minutes, until tender. Drain well, squeeze out the excess water, and set aside.

Set aside the duck legs for 5 minutes and keep warm. Skim off all but 4 tablespoons of the fat and cooking juices and pour into a large skillet over medium heat. Add the kale, season with salt and pepper, and stir for 3–5 minutes, until hot. Serve the duck with the turnips and kale.

Muscat-Poached pears

Method

Cut a sheet of parchment paper in a circle the same diameter as a heavy-bottom saucepan large enough to hold the 4 pears. Add the sugar, wine, and water to the pan and place over a medium heat, stirring occasionally until the sugar has dissolved.

Meanwhile, peel the pears, keeping the stems intact. Add the pears to the pan and reduce the heat to medium–low. Add the vanilla bean and orange zest, and lay the sheet of parchment paper on top. Cover the pan with the lid and let the pears poach for 20 minutes, or until tender.

Transfer the pears to a serving bowl using a slotted spoon. Bring the poaching liquid to a rapid boil and boil, without stirring, for 15 minutes, or until reduced and thick.

Serve the pears warm with the hot syrup spooned over and with sour cream, if using.

Ingredients
Serves 4

¾ cup sugar

1¼ cups California Muscat wine

1¼ cups water

4 dessert pears, such as Bartlett or Bosc

1 vanilla bean, split

1 long strip orange zest, white pith removed

sour cream, to serve (optional)

Soft-Centered chocolate cake

Ingredients

Makes 4

½ cup superfine sugar

¾ cup butter, plus extra for greasing

6 oz/175 g semisweet chocolate

3 large eggs

3 large egg yolks

1 tbsp all-purpose flour

mint leaves, to decorate

Method

Grease 4 dariole molds thoroughly with butter.

Fill a small saucepan halfway with water and bring it to simmering point. Place a heatproof bowl over the pan and add the sugar, butter, and chocolate. Stir until the butter has melted, then remove from the heat.

Whisk until well-mixed. Add the eggs and egg yolks and whisk them in. Sift in the flour and fold it in.

Pour the mixture into the molds and put them into the refrigerator for 30 minutes.

Preheat the oven to 425°F/220°C. Put the molds into the oven and bake for 8–10 minutes, then remove. Let rest, then turn out onto serving plates. Decorate each cake with mint leaves and serve.

Meyer lemon pots de crème with raspberry sauce

Ingredients

Makes 4

1¼ cups heavy cream

1 tsp freshly grated Meyer lemon zest

3 large eggs

1 large egg yolk

¾ cup superfine sugar

½ cup freshly squeezed Meyer lemon juice

RASPBERRY SAUCE

⅓ cup raspberries

2 tsp superfine sugar

squeeze of lemon juice

Method

Put the cream and lemon zest in a small saucepan over medium heat until small bubbles appear around the edge. Remove the pan from the heat, cover, and let steep for 20 minutes.

Preheat the oven to 325°F/160°C. Put the eggs, egg yolk, and superfine sugar into a large bowl and beat together. Meanwhile, return the pan of cream and lemon zest to a simmer before pouring in the eggs and sugar mixture. Whisk constantly until the sugar dissolves and add in the lemon juice. Remove the pan from the heat and strain the mixture through a nylon strainer into a large measuring cup for easy pouring.

Put four ¾-cup pots de crème in a small roasting pan. Divide the mixture evenly between the pots, filling them to about ¼ inch/0.5 cm from the top, then pour in boiling water to halfway up the sides of the pots.

Put the pan in the preheated oven and bake for 35–40 minutes, until just set. Remove from the pan and let cool completely, then cover and chill for 2–24 hours.

Meanwhile, make the sauce. Puree the raspberries and stir in the sugar until it dissolves. Add a splash of lemon juice.

Serve the lemon pots with a drizzle of the sauce on top and the remainder on the side.

NEW YORK

New Yorkers enjoy the world on their plates. Whatever cuisine you are in the mood to sample, chances are it is being prepared somewhere in the five boroughs that make up New York City. The contribution of generations of immigrants from all corners of the globe is evident on menus all around the town. Many dishes, such as the iconic New York Cheesecake, that are regarded as "typically New York" by the rest of the country, have their origins in Eastern Europe. The city's restaurant culture offers some of the most sophisticated dining in the United States, as well as the more relaxed, less expensive delis, with their unbeatable two-fisted sandwiches, meal-size salads, and Clam Chowder, an all-American favorite. New York cooking definitely offers something for everyone.

THE REUBEN SANDWICH

Ingredients

Serves 2

2 tbsp margarine, softened

4 slices of rye bread

4–6 oz/115–175 g cooked salt beef, thinly sliced

7 oz/200 g bottled sauerkraut, drained

1 cup grated Gruyère cheese

vegetable oil, for frying

pickled gherkins, to serve

thousand island dressing

2 tbsp mayonnaise

2 tbsp ketchup or chili sauce

1 medium green bell pepper, seeded and finely chopped

2 tbsp finely chopped pimento

2 tbsp finely chopped pickled gherkins

Method

To make the dressing, mix the ingredients together in a bowl until well blended.

Spread the margarine on one side of each slice of bread and lay margarine-side down. Spread the other sides with 1 tablespoon of the dressing.

Divide the salt beef between 2 slices of the bread, tucking in the sides to fit. Divide the sauerkraut and make an even layer on top of the salt beef, before covering with the grated cheese. Top with the remaining slices of bread, margarine-side facing up, and press firmly to compress the layers.

Heat a nonstick grill pan over medium–high heat and carefully slide the sandwiches into the pan. Using a spatula, press down on the tops of the sandwiches. Cook for 3 minutes, or until the undersides are crisp and golden. Carefully turn over the sandwiches, press down again, and cook for another 2 minutes, or until golden, the cheese is melted, and the salt beef is hot. Remove from the heat and transfer the sandwiches to a cutting board. Cut in half and serve with pickled gherkins.

POTATO KNISHES

Method

To make the pastry, put the flour, baking powder, and salt into a blender and pulse to combine. Add the butter and blend until fine breadcrumbs form. Spoon in the sour cream and blend again until a dough begins to form. Do not let the dough form a ball or the pastry will be tough.

Turn out the pastry onto a lightly floured work surface and knead lightly. Form into a ball and flatten into a circular shape. Wrap in plastic wrap and refrigerate for at least 2 hours.

To prepare the filling, heat the butter in a skillet over medium heat. Add the onions and cook for 15 minutes, or until soft and golden, stirring frequently. Remove from the heat, stir in the potatoes, and let cool slightly before adding the egg along with salt and pepper to taste. Let cool completely.

On a lightly floured work surface, roll out the pastry to about ⅛ inch/3 mm inch thick. Cut the pastry into 4-inch/10-cm squares and place a tablespoon of the filling in the center of each. Brush the edges with a little beaten egg and fold the bottom left corner up to the top right corner to form a triangle. Press to seal. Reroll any pastry scraps and continue forming triangles with the remaining dough and filling. Refrigerate for 30 minutes.

Preheat the oven to 400°F/200°C. Arrange the triangles 1 inch/2.5 cm apart on 2 large nonstick baking sheets. Brush with beaten egg and pierce the top of each triangle. Bake in batches for 20 minutes, or until puffed and golden. Cool on a wire rack and serve.

Ingredients

Makes 24

pastry

2½ cups all-purpose flour, sifted, plus extra for dusting

1 tsp baking powder

½ tsp salt

½ cup unsalted butter, cut into small cubes

½ cup sour cream

1 egg, beaten, for glazing

filling

2 tbsp butter or oil

2 onions, finely chopped

2–3 large potatoes, cooked, drained, and mashed

1 egg, beaten

salt and pepper

CLAM CHOWDER

Ingredients

Serves 4

2 lb/900 g clams

4 bacon strips, chopped

2 tbsp butter

1 onion, chopped

1 tbsp chopped fresh thyme

1 large potato, diced

1¼ cups milk

1 bay leaf

1⅔ cups heavy cream

1 tbsp chopped fresh parsley

salt and pepper

Method

Scrub the clams and put them into a large pan with a splash of water. Cook over high heat for 3–4 minutes, until they open. Discard any that remain closed. Strain, reserving the cooking liquid. Set aside until cool enough to handle, reserving 8 for a garnish.

Remove the clams from their shells, chopping them roughly if large, and set aside.

In a clean pan, fry the bacon until browned and crisp. Drain on paper towels. Add the butter to the same pan, and when it has melted, add the onion. Pan-fry for 4–5 minutes, until soft but not colored. Add the thyme and cook briefly before adding the diced potato, reserved clam cooking liquid, milk, and bay leaf. Bring to a boil and simmer for 10 minutes, or until the potato is just tender.

Discard the bay leaf, then transfer to a food processor and blend until smooth, or push through a strainer into a bowl.

Add the clams, bacon, and cream. Simmer for another 2–3 minutes, until heated through. Season to taste with salt and pepper. Stir in the chopped parsley and serve, garnished with the reserved clams in their shells.

BAGELS

Ingredients

Makes 12

1 tbsp active dry yeast

2 tbsp sugar

3½ tbsp vegetable oil, plus extra for oiling

1 tsp salt

1 cup warm water

3½ cups strong or all-purpose flour, plus extra for dusting

1 egg, beaten

1 egg beaten with ¼ tsp salt, for glazing

poppy and sesame seeds, for sprinkling

filling

smoked salmon

cream cheese

Method

Combine the yeast and half the sugar in a small bowl. Heat the remaining sugar, oil, salt, and water in a small pan for 1–2 minutes, or until warm and the sugar has dissolved, stirring. Pour into the yeast mixture. Cover with a dish towel and let stand for 5–7 minutes, or until the mixture begins to bubble. Put the flour into a food processor and, with the machine running, pour in the yeast mixture, then add the egg and process until a ball of dough forms. Add a little more flour if the dough is sticky; it should be smooth and elastic. Lightly oil a large bowl and add the ball of dough, turning to coat on all sides to prevent a crust from forming. Cover with the dish towel and let rise in a warm place for 1½–2 hours, or until doubled in volume.

Turn out onto a lightly floured work surface. Knead lightly to deflate. Divide the dough into 12 equal-size pieces. Roll each into a rope about 7 inches/18 cm long and shape into a ring. Wet one end and press firmly to seal. Arrange on a floured baking sheet, cover with the dish towel, and let rise for 25 minutes, or until doubled in volume.

Meanwhile, preheat the oven to 400°F/200°C. Lightly oil 2 large baking sheets. Bring a large pan of water to a boil. Working in batches, slide a few bagels into the water and cook for 1 minute. Remove to paper towels to drain. Arrange the bagels on the baking sheets and carefully brush with the egg mixture. Sprinkle half with sesame seeds and the remainder with poppy seeds. Bake for 12–15 minutes, or until golden and shiny. Remove to a wire rack to cool slightly.

Serve the bagels with smoked salmon and cream cheese.

BUFFALO WINGS

Ingredients

Makes 12

5 tbsp dark soy sauce

2 tbsp dry sherry

1 tbsp rice vinegar

juice of 1 orange and 2-inch/5-cm strip of orange rind, pith removed

1 tbsp dark brown sugar

1 star anise

1 tsp cornstarch, mixed to a paste with 3 tbsp water

1 tbsp finely chopped fresh ginger

1 tsp chili sauce

3 lb 5 oz/1.5 kg chicken wings

Method

Preheat the oven to 400°F/200°C. Place the soy sauce, sherry, vinegar, orange rind, sugar, and star anise into a pan, along with the juice extracted from the orange, and mix well.

Bring to a boil over medium heat, then stir in the cornstarch paste. Continue to boil, stirring constantly, for 1 minute, or until thickened. Remove the pan from the heat and stir in the ginger and chili sauce.

Remove and discard the tips from the chicken wings and place the wings in a single layer in an ovenproof dish or roasting pan. Pour the sauce over the wings, turning and stirring to coat.

Bake in the oven for 35–40 minutes, turning and basting with the sauce occasionally, until the chicken is tender and browned and the juices run clear when a skewer is inserted into the thickest part of the meat. Serve either hot or warm.

PIZZA SLICE

Ingredients

Serves 2

dough

1½ cups all-purpose flour, plus extra for dusting

1 tsp salt

1 tsp active dry yeast

1 tbsp olive oil, plus extra for brushing

6 tbsp lukewarm water

topping

6 tomatoes, sliced thinly

6 oz/175 g mozzarella cheese, drained and sliced thinly

salt and pepper

2 tbsp shredded fresh basil leaves

2 tbsp olive oil

Method

To make the pizza dough, sift the flour and salt into a bowl and stir in the yeast. Make a well in the center and pour in the oil and water. Gradually incorporate the dry ingredients into the liquid, using a wooden spoon or floured hands.

Turn out the dough onto a lightly floured counter and knead well for 5 minutes, until smooth and elastic. Return to the clean bowl, cover with lightly oiled plastic wrap, and set aside to rise in a warm place for about 1 hour, or until doubled in size.

Turn out the dough onto a lightly floured counter and punch down. Knead briefly, then cut it in half and roll out each piece into a circle about ¼ inch/ 5 mm thick. Transfer to a lightly oiled baking sheet and push up the edges with your fingers to form a small rim.

For the topping, arrange the tomato and mozzarella slices alternately over the pizza bases. Season to taste with salt and pepper, sprinkle with the basil, and drizzle with the olive oil.

Bake in a preheated oven, 450°F, for 15–20 minutes, until the crust is crisp and the cheese has melted. Cut into slices and serve.

NEW YORK STRIP STEAK WITH BÉARNAISE SAUCE

Ingredients

Serves 4

4 New York steaks, or entrecôte,
8 oz/225 g each

1 tbsp olive oil or clarified butter

salt and pepper

sautéed potatoes or French fries, to serve

Béarnaise sauce

large bunch of tarragon

1 shallot, finely chopped

generous ⅓ cup white wine vinegar

4 peppercorns

2 egg yolks

¾ cup butter, cut into small cubes

Method

Remove the steaks from the refrigerator
20 minutes before you intend to cook them.

To make the Béarnaise sauce, remove the
most tender leaves of the tarragon, finely
chop, and set aside. Roughly chop the
tougher parts and add them to a small
saucepan with the shallot, vinegar, and
peppercorns and simmer until it has reduced
to about 1 tablespoonful. Pass this through a
strainer into a clean heatproof bowl.

Bring a small saucepan of water to a boil,
place the bowl on top, and gently whisk in the
egg yolks until the mixture thickens a little.
Add the butter a piece at a time and whisk it
in until the sauce is thick. Add the chopped
tarragon leaves and mix in. Taste and add salt
if needed. Turn off the heat and cover to keep
warm while you cook the steaks.

Preheat the broiler to high with the broiler
pan underneath. Season the steaks with salt
and pepper and brush with the oil. Place the
steaks on the preheated pan and cook quickly
for 3–4 minutes on each side. Check that they
are nicely seared, then cover and let rest for
2 minutes before serving.

Stir the sauce in case it has separated. Serve
the steaks on lightly warmed plates with
potatoes and the sauce spooned over.

FUNNEL CAKES

Ingredients

Makes 4–6

1 cup all-purpose flour

1 tsp baking powder

½ tsp salt

1 egg, beaten

½ cup milk

½ tsp vanilla extract

sunflower oil or corn oil, for deep-frying

confectioners' sugar, for dusting

Method

Sift the flour, baking powder, and salt into a large bowl and make a well in the middle. Beat the egg with the milk and vanilla extract, then slowly stir it into the dry ingredients until a thick, free-flowing batter forms.

Meanwhile, heat at least 2 inches/ 5 cm of oil in a heavy-bottom skillet to 375°F/190°C, or until a cube of bread browns in 40 seconds.

Spoon one quarter of the mixture into a funnel, holding a finger over the hole. Let the batter fall into the hot oil in a continuous, spiraling circle until 5–6 inches/12.5–15 cm across, or let it fall in a haphazard fashion to form a lacelike circle; the batter will fall to the bottom of the pan and then rise to the surface. Fry for 1–2 minutes, until golden brown on the bottom. Turn carefully using 2 forks or long-handled spoons and fry until golden brown on the other side.

Remove from the oil and drain on folded paper towels. Let cool for a few seconds, then dust thickly with confectioners' sugar. Serve at once, then repeat until all the batter has been used.

VANILLA GELATO

Ingredients

Serves 6–8

scant 2 cups whole milk

1 vanilla bean

6 egg yolks

⅔ cup superfine sugar

Method

Pour the milk into a large heavy-bottom pan. Split open the vanilla bean and scrape out the seeds into the milk, then add the whole vanilla bean. Bring almost to a boil, then remove from the heat and let stand for 30 minutes. Remove the vanilla bean from the milk.

Put the egg yolks and sugar in a large bowl and whisk together until pale and the mixture leaves a trail when the whisk is lifted. Gradually add the milk, stirring constantly with a wooden spoon.

Strain the mixture into the rinsed-out pan or a double boiler and cook over low heat for 10–15 minutes, stirring constantly, until the mixture thickens slightly. Do not let the mixture boil or it will curdle. Remove the custard from the heat and let cool for at least 1 hour, stirring occasionally to prevent a skin from forming.

If using an ice-cream machine, churn the mixture in the machine following the manufacturer's instructions. Alternatively, freeze the custard in a freezerproof container, uncovered, for 1–2 hours, or until it begins to set around the edges. Turn the custard into a bowl and stir with a fork or beat in a food processor until smooth. Return to the freezer and repeat the breaking up of the ice crystals every 30 minutes for 2 hours. Return to the freezer until firm or required. Cover the container with a lid for storing.

New York Cheesecake

Ingredients

Serves 10

generous ½ cup butter, plus extra for greasing

1¾ cups finely crushed graham crackers

1 tbsp granulated sugar

2 lb/900 g cream cheese

1¼ cups superfine sugar

2 tbsp all-purpose flour

1 tsp vanilla extract

finely grated zest of 1 orange

finely grated zest of 1 lemon

3 eggs

2 egg yolks

1¼ cups heavy cream

Method

Preheat the oven to 350°F/180°C. Place a small saucepan over low heat, add the butter, and heat until it melts, then remove from the heat, stir in the crushed crackers and sugar, and mix thoroughly. Press the cracker mixture tightly into the bottom of a 9-inch/23-cm springform cake pan. Place in the oven and bake for 10 minutes. Remove from the oven and let cool on a wire rack.

Increase the oven temperature to 400°F/200°C. With an electric food mixer beat the cream cheese until creamy, then gradually add the sugar and flour and beat until smooth. Increase the speed and beat in the vanilla extract, orange zest, and lemon zest, then beat in the eggs and egg yolks one at a time. Finally, beat in the cream. Scrape any excess from the sides and beaters of the mixer into the mixture. It should be light and whippy—beat on a faster setting if you need to.

Grease the sides of the cake pan and pour in the filling. Smooth the top, transfer to the preheated oven, and bake for 15 minutes, then reduce the temperature to 200°F/100°C and bake for an additional 30 minutes. Turn off the oven and let the cheesecake stand in it for 2 hours to cool and set. Cover and refrigerate overnight.

Slide a knife around the edge of the cake, then unfasten the pan, cut the cheesecake into wedge-shape slices, and serve.

London

England's capital offers a stunning variety of cooking and food, with immigrant communities bringing global flavors that sit comfortably alongside more traditional dishes. In twenty-first-century London, chicken tikka masala and shish kebabs are as much "typically" London fare as are classic favorites, such as Bubble & Squeak and Fish & Chips. The popularity of gastro pubs—slightly cheaper alternatives to restaurants—give young chefs a chance to showcase their talent and reach celebrity status, while domestic cooks shop at Borough Market, a popular foodie destination, as well as a network of smaller weekly farmers' markets throughout the city. Yet, amid the fast pace of the modern city, it is still possible to stop for a leisurely afternoon tea, an enduring tradition featuring freshly baked scones.

Full English breakfast

Ingredients

Serves 1

2 good-quality pork sausages

2–3 smoked Canadian bacon slices

1 egg

1 slice 2-day-old whole wheat bread (optional)

1 large tomato, halved

vegetable oil, to drizzle

2–3 mushrooms

salt and pepper

Method

Place the sausages under a hot broiler and broil for about 15–20 minutes, turning frequently, until they are well browned. Meanwhile, place the bacon slices in a dry skillet and fry for 2–4 minutes on each side, depending on how crispy you like your bacon. Remove from the skillet, leaving all the excess bacon fat, and keep the bacon warm.

Using the same skillet used for the bacon, break the egg into the pan. Fry for a few seconds until the white sets, then baste with the fat to make sure it is evenly cooked, with the white completely set and the yolk remaining soft in the center. Remove the egg from the skillet using a wooden spatula and let it rest on a paper towel to absorb any excess fat.

Place the bread, if using, in the bacon fat in the same skillet and cook for 1–2 minutes on one side, then turn over and repeat. Do not cook too quickly or the bread will burn. Set aside and keep warm.

The tomato halves can be placed under the hot broiler with the sausages. Drizzle with a little oil, and season to taste with salt and pepper before broiling for 3–4 minutes. The mushrooms can be broiled with the tomatoes or quickly fried in the skillet with a little extra oil added. Arrange the sausages, bacon, egg, fried bread (if using), tomato halves, and mushrooms on a large hot platter and serve at once.

Kippers

Ingredients

Serves 1

1 kipper

pat of butter

pepper

*buttered whole wheat bread, and lemon wedges,
to serve*

Method

Place the kipper in a skillet and cover with water.

Bring to a boil, then reduce the heat, cover, and simmer gently for about 5 minutes.

Drain on paper towels and place on a warm plate with a pat of butter on top and some pepper to taste.

Serve immediately with the buttered whole wheat bread and a squeeze of lemon juice.

Fish and chips

Ingredients

Serves 2

vegetable oil, for deep-frying

3 large floury potatoes

2 thick cod or haddock fillets, 6 oz/175 g each

1¼ cups self-rising flour, plus extra for dusting

scant 1 cup cold lager

salt and pepper

tartar sauce, to serve

Method

Heat the oil in a temperature-controlled deep fat fryer to 250°F/120°C, or in a heavy-bottom saucepan, checking the temperature with a thermometer, to blanch the fries (these are the "chips"). Preheat the oven to 300°F/150°C.

Peel the potatoes and cut into even-size fries. Fry for about 8–10 minutes, depending on size, until softened but not colored. Remove from the oil, drain on paper towels, and place in a warm dish in the oven. Increase the temperature of the oil to 350–375°F/180–190°C, or until a cube of bread browns in 30 seconds.

Meanwhile, season the fish with salt and pepper, and dust it lightly with a little flour.

Make a thick batter by sifting the flour into a bowl with a little salt and whisking in most of the lager. Check the consistency before adding the remainder; it should be very thick like heavy cream. Dip one fillet into the batter and let the batter coat it thickly. Carefully place the fish in the hot oil, then repeat with the other fillet. Cook for 8–10 minutes, depending on the thickness of the fish. Turn the fillets over halfway through the cooking time. Remove the fish from the fryer or saucepan, drain, and keep warm.

Make sure the oil temperature is still at 350°F/180°C and return the fries to the fryer or saucepan. Cook for another 2–3 minutes, until golden brown and crispy. Drain and season with salt and pepper before serving with the battered fish and tartar sauce.

Steak and kidney pie

Ingredients

Serves 4

butter, for greasing

1 lb/450 g braising steak, trimmed and cut into 1-inch/2.5-cm pieces

2 lambs' kidneys, cored and cut into 1-inch/ 2.5-cm pieces

generous ⅓ cup all-purpose flour

1 onion, finely chopped

4 oz /115 g large portobello mushrooms, sliced (optional)

1 tbsp chopped fresh parsley

about 1¼ cups stock, or a mixture of beer and water

salt and pepper

suet pastry

2½ cups self-rising flour

1½ cups suet

1 cup cold water

salt and pepper

Method

Grease a 1-quart/1.2 liter ovenproof bowl.

Put the prepared meat into a large plastic bag with the flour and salt and pepper, and shake well until all the meat is well coated. Add the onion, mushrooms, if using, and the parsley, and shake again.

Make the suet pastry by mixing the flour, suet, and some salt and pepper together. Add enough of the cold water to make a soft dough. Keep one quarter of the dough to one side and roll the remainder out to form a circle big enough to line the ovenproof bowl. Line the bowl, making sure that there is a good ½ inch/1 cm hanging over the edge. Place the meat mixture in the bowl and pour in enough of the stock to cover the meat. Roll out the remaining pastry to make a lid. Fold in the edges of the pastry, dampen them, and place the lid on top. Seal firmly in place.

Cover with a piece of wax paper and then foil, with a pleat to allow for expansion during cooking, and seal well. Place in a steamer or large saucepan filled halfway with boiling water.

Simmer the pie for 4–5 hours, adding extra water from time to time. Remove the bowl from the steamer and take off the coverings. Wrap a clean cloth around the bowl and serve.

Bubble and squeak

Ingredients

Serves 2–3

1 lb/450 g green cabbage

1 onion, thinly sliced

4 tbsp olive oil

salt and pepper

mashed potato

1 lb/450 g floury potatoes,
peeled and cut into chunks

4 tbsp butter

3 tbsp hot milk

salt and pepper

Method

To make the mashed potato, cook the potatoes in a large saucepan of boiling salted water for 15–20 minutes. Drain well, and mash with a potato masher until smooth. Season with salt and pepper, add the butter and milk, and stir well.

Cut the cabbage into quarters, remove the center stalk, and shred the leaves finely. In a large skillet, fry the onion in half the oil until soft. Add the cabbage to the skillet and stir fry for 2–3 minutes, until softened. Season with salt and pepper, add the mashed potato, and mix together well. Press the mixture firmly into the skillet and let cook over a high heat for 4–5 minutes, so that the bottom is golden. Place a plate over the skillet and invert the skillet so that the potato cake falls onto the plate. Add the remaining oil to the skillet, reheat, and slip the cake back into the skillet with the uncooked side down.

Continue to cook for another 5 minutes until the other side is golden, too. Turn out onto a hot plate and cut into wedges for serving. Serve at once.

Cauliflower cheese

Method

Cook the cauliflower in a saucepan of boiling salted water for 4–5 minutes. It should still be firm. Drain, place in a hot 1¼-quart/1.4-liter gratin bowl and keep warm.

Melt the butter in the rinsed-out saucepan over a medium heat and stir in the flour. Cook for 1 minute, stirring continuously. Remove from the heat and stir in the milk gradually until you have a smooth consistency.

Return to a low heat and continue to stir while the sauce comes to a boil and thickens. Reduce the heat and simmer gently, stirring constantly, for about 3 minutes, until the sauce is creamy and smooth.

Remove from the heat and stir in the cheddar cheese and a good grating of the nutmeg. Taste and season well with salt and pepper. Pour the hot sauce over the cauliflower, top with the Parmesan, and place under a hot broiler to brown. Serve immediately.

Ingredients

Serves 4

1 large cauliflower, trimmed and cut into florets (1 lb 8 oz/675 g prepared weight)

1½ oz/40 g oz butter

generous ¼ cup all-purpose flour

2 cups milk

1 cup finely grated cheddar cheese

whole nutmeg, for grating

1 tbsp grated Parmesan cheese

salt and pepper

Roast pork belly

Ingredients

Serves 4

15 dried bay leaves

five 1-inch/2.5-cm pieces
fresh ginger, grated

15 garlic cloves, peeled and roughly chopped

generous ⅓ cup olive oil

½ tsp pepper

2 tsp salt

1 tbsp whole cardamom seeds, cracked
(optional)

6 lb 8 oz/3 kg pork spareribs, complete with
skin and bones (make sure there are 8 ribs),
skin scored with a knife about
every ½ inch/1 cm

Method

Combine all of the ingredients, except the pork, in a small food processor, or mash using a large pestle and mortar, until a thick paste forms. Put the pork spareribs into a roasting pan that will fit in your refrigerator, then rub the paste into it on all sides, making sure you get some into the cuts through the fat. Now put it in the refrigerator for at least 1 hour and up to 2 days.

Preheat the oven to 325°F/160°C. Place the pork, uncovered, in the oven and roast for 2 hours. Increase the oven temperature to 475°F/240°C and cook for an additional 20–30 minutes to crisp the skin, checking every 10 minutes to make sure that the pork doesn't burn.

If the pork skin hasn't turned into good cracklings by now, heat the broiler to high and place the pork under the broiler, making sure that it doesn't burn. Cut off the cracklings in one large piece and set aside, uncovered. Cover the meat with foil and let rest for 15 minutes before serving. Cut it at the table, giving each person a whole rib and a chunk of cracklings.

Sticky toffee pudding

Ingredients

Serves 4

generous 1 cup finely chopped, pitted dates

1 tsp baking soda

generous ⅔ cup water

scant ¾ cup butter, plus extra for greasing

1 cup superfine sugar

2 eggs

1 tsp vanilla extract

1¾ cups self-rising flour

sauce

¾ cup dark brown sugar

2 tbsp butter, cut into chunks

¼ cup heavy cream

Method

Preheat the oven to 350°F/180°C. Put the dates, baking soda, and water in a saucepan and simmer for 5 minutes until the dates are softened. Set aside.

Beat the butter with the golden superfine sugar until light and fluffy, then beat in the eggs, vanilla extract, and flour, then the dates and their cooking liquid. Grease an 8-inch/ 20-cm round cake pan or baking dish with a little butter and add the mixture. Cook for about 35 minutes, checking after 20 minutes that it isn't burning. It is ready when a knife inserted into the center comes out clean. Be careful that it does not dry out.

Meanwhile, to make the sauce, put the brown sugar, butter, and cream into a saucepan and stir over low heat until fully mixed. Increase the heat and boil for 1 minute to thicken. Remove from the heat and keep warm. To serve, place a piece of sponge on each of 4 plates and top with the sauce.

Scones

Ingredients

Makes 10–12

3¼ cups all-purpose flour,
plus extra for dusting

½ tsp salt

2 tsp baking powder

4 tbsp butter

2 tbsp superfine sugar

generous 1 cup milk, plus 3 tbsp for glazing

strawberry preserve and whipped cream,
to serve

Method

Preheat the oven to 425°F/220°C.

Sift the flour, salt, and baking powder into a bowl. Rub in the butter until the mixture resembles breadcrumbs. Stir in the sugar.

Make a well in the center and pour in the milk. Stir in using a round-bladed knife and make a soft dough. Turn the mixture onto a floured surface and lightly flatten the dough until it is of an even thickness, about ½ inch/1 cm. Don't be heavy handed—scones need a light touch.

Use a 2½-inch/6-cm pastry cutter to cut out the scones and place on the baking sheet. Glaze with a little milk and bake for 10–12 minutes, until golden and well risen. Cool on a wire rack and serve freshly baked with strawberry preserve and whipped cream.

Spotted dick with custard

Ingredients

Serves 6

scant 1⅔ cups self-rising flour, plus extra for dusting

½ cup lard

generous ¼ cup superfine sugar

generous ¾ cup golden raisins

grated rind of 1 lemon

⅔–¾ cup milk

2 tsp melted butter, for greasing

custard

generous 1¾ cups light cream

5 egg yolks

3 tbsp superfine sugar

½ tsp vanilla extract

1 tsp cornstarch (optional)

Method

Mix together the flour, lard, sugar, golden raisins, and lemon rind in a mixing bowl. Pour in the milk and stir together to form a fairly soft dough.

Turn out onto a floured surface and roll into a cylinder. Wrap in wax paper that has been well-buttered and seal the ends, allowing room for the pudding to rise. Overwrap with foil and place in a steamer over a saucepan of boiling water.

Steam for about 1–1½ hours, checking the water level in the saucepan from time to time.

To make the custard, heat the cream in a small saucepan just to boiling point. Cream the egg yolks, sugar, and vanilla extract together in a measuring cup. You can add the cornstarch to this cold egg yolk mixture to ensure the sauce does not separate. Pour the hot cream into the cup, stirring all the time. Return the mixture to the saucepan.

Heat the custard very gently, stirring constantly, until the sauce has just thickened, then remove from the heat. Alternatively, you can cook the custard in a bowl over a saucepan of simmering water to prevent overcooking.

Remove the pudding from the steamer and unwrap. Place on a hot plate and cut into thick slices. Serve with plenty of custard.

PARIS

Paris and fine dining is a timeless partnership. From Michelin-starred restaurants that set the benchmark for chefs around the world, to small corner bistros, with their gingham tablecloths, chalkboard menus, carafes of house wine, and simple meals, it is difficult not to be seduced by the City of Light's enduring food culture. Young chefs might experiment with fusion cooking and edgy flavor combinations, but most Parisian cooks stick with tradition, preparing classics, such as Soupe de Poissons, Cassoulet, Crème Brûlée, and Crepes Suzette, exactly as their grandparents did. Covered and open-air markets dotted throughout the city, the food halls in large department stores, and thousands of small, independent food stores, make shopping for and cooking food in Paris as enjoyable as dining.

SOUPE DE POISSONS WITH ROUILLE

Ingredients

Serves 6–8

generous ⅓ cup olive oil

3 onions, roughly chopped

3 carrots, roughly chopped

3 celery stalks, roughly chopped

1 fennel bulb, finely chopped

6 garlic cloves, roughly chopped

1 bay leaf

⅔ cup Vermouth

2 sprigs thyme

2 lb 4 oz/1 kg whole whitefish, cleaned and filleted, bones reserved

4 lb 8 oz/2 kg bones from whitefish or shellfish (ask your fish dealer)

9 oz/250 g unpeeled shrimp

11¼ cups water

juice and zest of 1 orange

pinch of saffron

toasted slices of baguette and grated Parmesan cheese, to serve

Rouille

½ cup fresh breadcrumbs soaked in 1 tbsp water

3 garlic cloves, roughly chopped

1 egg yolk

1 red chile, seeded and chopped

½ tsp salt

generous ¾ cup olive oil

Method

Place a large saucepan over medium heat and add the olive oil. Add the onions, carrots, celery, fennel, garlic, and bay leaf and cook gently for 20 minutes, until softened. Add the Vermouth and thyme and simmer for 2 minutes.

Add the fish, fish bones, and shrimp and increase the heat. Cook, stirring, for 5 minutes, then add the water, orange juice and zest, and saffron. Bring to a boil and simmer for 45 minutes.

Meanwhile, make the rouille. Put all of the ingredients except the olive oil into a food processor and blend to a paste. Keep blending and add the olive oil in a slow stream until the consistency is that of a thick mayonnaise. Put in the refrigerator to chill.

Crush the bones by liquidizing the soup in batches (including bones, shells, and heads), or by using a potato masher and hammer in the saucepan. Let stand for 20 minutes. Strain through a colander first, then through a fine strainer, then pour into a saucepan. Taste and season and heat again, ready to serve.

Serve in bowls with slices of toasted baguette, bowls of rouille, and some grated Parmesan cheese to float on the soup.

LEEK AND GOAT CHEESE CREPES

Ingredients

Makes 8

2 tbsp unsalted butter

½ tbsp sunflower oil

7 oz/200 g leeks, halved, rinsed, and finely shredded

freshly grated nutmeg, to taste

1 tbsp finely snipped fresh chives

8 savory crepes

3 oz/85 g soft goat cheese, rind removed if necessary, chopped

salt and pepper

Method

Preheat the oven to 400°F/200°C. Melt the butter with the oil in a heavy-bottom pan with a lid over medium–high heat. Add the leeks and stir around so that they are well coated. Stir in salt and pepper to taste, but remember the cheese might be salty. Add a few gratings of nutmeg, then cover the leeks with a sheet of wet wax paper and put the lid on the pan. Reduce the heat to very low and let the leeks sweat for 5–7 minutes, until very tender but not brown. Stir in the chives, then taste and adjust the seasoning if necessary.

Put 1 crepe on the counter and put one eighth of the leeks on the crepe. Top with one eighth of the cheese, then fold the crepe into a square pocket or simply roll it around the filling. Place the stuffed crepe on a baking sheet, then continue to fill and fold, or roll, the remaining crepes.

Put the baking sheet in the oven and bake for 5 minutes, or until the crepes are hot and the cheese starts to melt. Serve hot.

RILLETS

Ingredients

Makes about 3 lb 5 oz/1.5 kg

1 lb 2 oz/500 g pork shoulder

2 lb 4 oz/1 kg pork spareribs, rindless and boneless

1¼ cups pork fat or lard

2 cups water

1 bouquet garni of 2 sprigs thyme, 2 sprigs parsley, and 3 bay leaves, tied with string

1 clove

½ tsp allspice

grating of nutmeg

salt and pepper

to serve

gherkins

mustard

crusty bread

Method

Cut the meat into 2-inch/5-cm cubes, and chop the fat into ½-inch/1-cm cubes. Place the meat and fat in a large, heavy-bottom saucepan with the water, bouquet garni, and clove. (Do not add more water. The pork should collapse, not boil.)

Cover the pan and place it over the lowest heat your stove can create, using a heat diffuser if you've got one, or place it in a very low oven, 250°F/120°C. The pot should just be gently shuddering.

Cook for 4–6 hours, checking and stirring about every 30 minutes to make sure that it's not burning.

Remove from the heat and set aside to cool. Remove the bouquet garni and clove. While it's still slightly warm, add the spices and seasonings, then take two forks and gently tear apart the pork, mixing the fat with the meat. Be careful to keep the "planks" texture and avoid turning the meat into a paste.

Cover the meat with a piece of wax paper or plastic wrap and refrigerate for 2–3 days before serving (although you can eat them straight away). They will last for at least an additional week in the refrigerator, but if you put them into sterilized jars and spread a layer of melted lard on top, they will keep for months.

To serve, drop a spoonful onto a plate beside some gherkins, mustard, and crusty bread.

BOUILLABAISSE

Ingredients

Serves 8

2 lb 4 oz/1 kg selection of at least 4 different firm white fish fillets, such as red snapper, sea bass, eel, or monkfish, scaled and cleaned, but not skinned

generous ⅓ cup olive oil

2 onions, finely chopped

1 fennel bulb, finely chopped

4 garlic cloves, crushed

2 lb 6 oz/1.2 kg canned chopped plum tomatoes

6 cups fish stock

pinch saffron strands

grated zest of 1 orange

bouquet garni of 2 sprigs thyme, 2 sprigs parsley, and 2 bay leaves, tied together with string

1 lb 2 oz/500 g mussels, cleaned

1 lb 2 oz/500 g cooked shrimp, shell on

salt and pepper

crusty French baguette and rouille (see page 76), to serve

Method

Carefully bone the fish, then cut the fillets into bite-size pieces.

Heat the olive oil in a very large skillet or wide saucepan with a lid and gently fry the onion and fennel for about 15 minutes, until softened. Add the garlic and fry for 2 minutes, then add the tomatoes and simmer for 2 minutes. Add the stock, saffron, orange zest, and bouquet garni and bring to a boil. Simmer, uncovered, for 15 minutes.

Add the fish pieces, mussels, and shrimp and cover the skillet. Simmer for an additional 5–10 minutes, until the mussels have opened. Discard any that remain closed. Check the seasoning.

Serve with some crusty baguette and rouille.

CROQUE MONSIEUR

Method

Preheat the broiler to high. Lay one piece of bread buttered-side up and place the ham on top. Cover with two thirds of the cheese and season. Lay the other slice of bread on top, buttered-side down. Brush the top side with the melted butter and place the bread, buttered-side up, under the broiler.

Broil until browned, then remove. Turn the sandwich over and scatter the remaining cheese on top. Replace under the broiler and cook until the cheese is bubbling and browned. Remove and serve with salad greens.

Ingredients

Serves 1

2 slices white bread, buttered

2 slices smoked ham

½ cup grated Gruyère cheese

pat of butter, melted

salt and pepper

mixed salad greens, to serve

RATATOUILLE

Ingredients

Serves 4

3 red bell peppers

generous ¾ cup olive oil

1 zucchini, thickly sliced

1 fennel bulb, roughly chopped

2 large red onions, roughly sliced

3 white onions, thickly sliced

2 large eggplants, thickly sliced

1 lb 5 oz/600 g ripe tomatoes, blanched, peeled, cored, and seeded

1 large tbsp fresh thyme leaves

1 large tbsp fresh rosemary leaves

1 tsp sugar

salt and pepper

crusty bread and butter, to serve

Method

Preheat the broiler to high, then place the red bell peppers on the broiler pan and place under the heat until the skins blacken. Turn and broil again, continuing until they are blackened all over. Put them in a bowl and cover with plastic wrap to sweat for 10 minutes, then peel them under cold running water. Cut them open and seed them, then chop the flesh into large chunks.

Meanwhile, place a large heavy-bottom saucepan over medium heat and add half the oil. Add the zucchini and fry until it begins to brown. Transfer it to a large roasting pan and keep warm. Add the fennel and onions to the pan and fry for 15–20 minutes, until they soften, then transfer them to the roasting pan. Add the eggplants and some more oil (they will soak up a lot) and fry until they begin to brown. Add them to the roasting pan, laid flat in a single layer.

Preheat the oven to 375°F/190°C. Add the tomatoes, red bell peppers, thyme, and rosemary to the roasting pan and distribute the vegetables evenly across it. Sprinkle the sugar over the whole lot and gently mix through. There should be one layer of vegetables, not a stew. If you need more room, use two roasting pans. Season with salt and pepper, drizzle with olive oil, and place, uncovered, in the preheated oven for 40–50 minutes, until they start to brown.

Refrigerate overnight or eat immediately with crusty bread and butter.

CASSOULET

Method

Drain and rinse the beans and put them in a large saucepan with the bouquet garni, celery, onion quarters, whole garlic, and seasoning. Add the water and bring to a boil. Skim off any foam, then reduce the heat to low. Gently simmer for 1 hour, uncovered.

Meanwhile, cut the meat into pieces 1½ inches/4 cm square, then add the duck fat to a large heavy-bottom saucepan and place over high heat. Add the bacon and brown it all over. Remove and reserve, then repeat with the sausages, then the lamb. Add the sliced onions, chopped garlic, and tomato paste and cook in the remaining fat for 2 minutes. Remove from the heat and let cool.

Preheat the oven to 350°F/180°C. Drain the beans, reserving the liquid but discarding the vegetables. In a large casserole dish, layer beans and meat alternately. Add the fried onion-and-tomato paste mixture, and enough of the bean-cooking liquid to almost cover the beans. Sprinkle over the breadcrumbs and cook in the oven, covered, for 1 hour. Reduce the oven temperature to 275°F/140°C, remove the cover, and cook for an additional hour.

Check that it's not too dry, adding a little heated bean liquid or water if necessary. Stir the crust into the top of the cassoulet and serve with a green salad.

Ingredients

Serves 8

1 lb 2 oz/500 g dried navy beans, soaked overnight

bouquet garni of 4 sprigs parsley, 2 sprigs thyme, and 4 bay leaves, tied with string

1 celery stalk, roughly chopped

3 onions, 1 quartered, 2 thinly sliced

4 large garlic cloves, 2 whole, 2 chopped

8 cups water

1 lb 2 oz/500 g thick-cut bacon, cut into large chunks

2 tbsp duck fat or vegetable oil

14 oz/400 g Toulouse sausage or pork sausage, sliced

14 oz/400 g lamb shoulder, boned and cut into 4 large chunks

2 tbsp tomato paste

1¼ cups fresh breadcrumbs

salt and pepper

fresh green salad, to serve

CRÈME BRÛLÉE

Ingredients

Serves 8

2¼ cups heavy cream

1 vanilla bean

½ cup superfine sugar, plus extra
for the topping

6 egg yolks

Method

Preheat the oven to 325°F/160°C.

Pour the cream into a small saucepan. Split the vanilla bean in half lengthwise. Scrape the seeds into the pan, then chop the bean into little pieces and add that too. Heat the cream to boiling, then reduce the heat and simmer gently for 5 minutes.

Put the sugar and egg yolks in a heatproof bowl and beat with a spoon until well mixed. Pour the hot cream into the egg mixture, beating (not whisking) as you pour, until it's nicely thickened. Pass this mixture through a fine strainer into another bowl or pitcher. Pour the mixture into a wide, flat dish (or 8 small shallow dishes) and lay this in a roasting pan. Carefully pour some boiling hot water into the pan so that it comes halfway up the sides of the crème brûlée dish or dishes.

Place in the preheated oven and bake for 33–45 minutes, until the custard has just set.

Remove from the oven and let cool to room temperature. Sprinkle over some sugar and then gently caramelize it using a kitchen blowtorch, or under a very hot broiler. Let cool for a few minutes, then serve.

CREPE SUZETTE

Ingredients

Serves 4

8 sweet crepes

2 tbsp brandy

orange sauce

¼ cup superfine sugar

1 tbsp water

finely grated rind of 1 large orange

½ cup freshly squeezed orange juice

½ stick unsalted butter, diced

1 tbsp Cointreau, Grand Marnier, or other orange-flavored liqueur

Method

To make the orange sauce, place the sugar in a wide sauté pan or skillet over medium heat and stir in the water. Continue stirring until the sugar dissolves, then increase the heat to high and let the syrup bubble for 1–2 minutes, or until it begins to turn golden brown.

Stir in the orange rind and juice, then add the butter and continue stirring until it melts. Stir in the orange-flavored liqueur.

Lay one of the crepes flat in the sauté pan and spoon the sauce over. Using a fork and the spoon, fold the crepe into quarters and push to the side of the pan. Add the next crepe to the pan and repeat. Continue until all the crepes are coated with the sauce and folded. Remove the pan from the heat.

Warm the brandy in a ladle or small pan, ignite, and pour over the crepes to flambé while shaking the pan.

When the flames die down, serve the crepes with the sauce spooned over.

TARTE TATIN

Method

Place an 8-inch/20-cm ovenproof skillet over low heat and add the sugar. Melt the sugar until it starts to caramelize, but do not let it burn, then add the butter and stir it in to make a light taffy sauce. Remove from the heat.

Peel the apples and cut them into eighths vertically. Core the apples and lay them in the skillet on top of the sauce, cut-side up. They should fill the skillet. If there are any large gaps, add a few more apple pieces. Place the skillet over medium heat and cover. Simmer, without stirring, for about 5–10 minutes, until the apples have soaked up some of the sauce, then remove from the heat.

Preheat the oven to 375°F/190°C. Roll out the pastry so that it will thickly cover the skillet, with extra space on the sides. Lay it on top of the apples and tuck the edges down inside between the fruit and the skillet until it is sealed. Don't worry about making it look too neat—it will be turned over before eating.

Put the skillet into the preheated oven and bake for 25–35 minutes, checking to make sure the pastry doesn't burn. The pastry should be puffed and golden. Remove from the oven and let rest for 30–60 minutes.

When you're ready to eat, make sure the tart is still a little warm (you can reheat it on the stove if necessary) and place a plate on top. Carefully turn it over and lift the skillet off. Serve with some vanilla ice cream.

Ingredients

Serves 6

1 cup superfine sugar

scant ¾ cup unsalted butter

1 lb 12 oz/800 g tart apples

12 oz/350 g store-bought puff pastry

vanilla ice cream, to serve

ROME

Roman menus are guided by the seasons and tradition.
Simple pasta dishes, broiled meats and fish, and fresh
vegetables lightly cooked in olive oil with garlic are the
backbone of la cucina romana, or the Roman kitchen.
Preparing top-quality ingredients with perfect simplicity is a
valued attribute for any Roman cook, be they professional or
domestic. Anyone looking for experimentation and novelty
while dining in the Eternal City will be greatly disappointed.
Instead, Romans take comfort in the predictable familiarity
of mealtimes throughout the year. In spring, for example,
young vegetables are celebrated with Risotto Primavera,
then, when the calendar moves on to summer, Italian Tomato
Soup features, giving way to comforting bowls of Ribollita
in winter. Strawberries in December is simply not the
Roman way.

ITALIAN TOMATO SOUP

Ingredients

Serves 6

10½ oz/300 g sourdough bread

generous ⅓ cup chicken stock

4 tbsp extra virgin olive oil

3 tbsp fresh sage leaves, shredded

4 garlic cloves, peeled and finely chopped

1 lb 12 oz/800 g canned peeled plum tomatoes

1 tsp sugar

1 cup hot water

½ cup grated Parmesan cheese

salt and pepper

Method

Chop the bread into rough chunks, about 1 inch/2.5 cm square. Place a heavy-bottom saucepan over medium heat. Add the stock, oil, and sage and simmer until reduced by half. Add the bread and garlic, increase the heat to high, and fry until all the liquid has been soaked up and the bread begins to become crispy.

Add the tomatoes and sugar, stir, and simmer for 15 minutes. Add hot water to thin the soup to your preferred consistency (it should be thick). Simmer for an additional minute. Taste and adjust the seasoning.

Ladle into bowls, sprinkle a little Parmesan cheese on top, and serve.

RIBOLLITA

Ingredients

Serves 4

3 tbsp olive oil

2 medium red onions, coarsely chopped

3 carrots, sliced

3 celery stalks, coarsely chopped

3 garlic cloves, chopped

1 tbsp chopped fresh thyme

14 oz/400 g canned cannellini beans, drained and rinsed

14 oz/400 g canned chopped tomatoes

2½ cups water or vegetable stock

2 tbsp chopped fresh parsley

1 lb 2 oz/500 g Tuscan kale or savoy cabbage, trimmed and sliced

1 small day-old ciabatta loaf, torn into small pieces

salt and pepper

extra virgin olive oil, to serve

Method

Heat the oil in a large saucepan and cook the onions, carrots, and celery for 10–15 minutes, stirring frequently. Add the garlic, thyme, and salt and pepper to taste. Continue to cook for an additional 1–2 minutes, until the vegetables are golden and caramelized.

Add the cannellini beans to the pan and pour in the tomatoes. Add enough of the water to cover the vegetables.

Bring to a boil and simmer for 20 minutes. Add the parsley and Tuscan kale and cook for an additional 5 minutes.

Stir in the bread and add a little more water, if needed. The soup should be thick.

Taste and adjust the seasoning, if needed. Ladle into warmed serving bowls and serve hot, drizzled with extra virgin olive oil.

TOASTED EGGPLANT & ANCHOVY FOCACCIA WITH GOAT CHEESE

Method

Preheat the broiler on a medium–high setting. Slice the focaccia in half horizontally and lay on the rack in the broiler pan. Toast the underside of the bread, and cut side of the top half, for about 2 minutes, until browned.

Drain and reserve the oil from the anchovies. Remove the bread and lay the eggplant slices on the rack. Brush with the reserved oil and broil for 4–5 minutes, until well browned.

Chop the anchovies and mix with the scallions. Arrange the eggplant slices and cheese on the bread, covering the untoasted surfaces of the bottom and the top of the loaf (or the tops of both flatbreads). Top with the anchovy mixture. Brush the remaining oil lightly over the eggplant. Broil for 3–4 minutes, until browned.

Puree the basil, cilantro, lemon zest, and olive oil in a blender. Top the bottom half of bread with tomatoes and add the other half on top, eggplant slices up. Cut into wedges. Serve drizzled with the herb oil.

Ingredients
Serves 4

1 thick focaccia loaf (about 6–7 inches/15–17 cm) or 2 Italian flatbreads

2 oz/55 g canned anchovies in olive oil

1 eggplant, about 9 oz/250 g, thinly sliced

6 scallions, chopped

5 oz/140 g goat cheese log, thinly sliced

handful of basil leaves

handful of fresh cilantro leaves

grated zest of 1 lemon

4 tbsp olive oil

10–12 cherry tomatoes, halved

SALTIMBOCCA

Method

Lay the pork chops on a cutting board and flatten them with a mallet or rolling pin until they are the same size as the ham slices. Lay down a piece of ham, put a piece of pork on top, and place a sage leaf at the edge nearest to you. Season with salt and pepper, then roll the meat around the sage leaf and secure it with a toothpick. The ham should be on the outside. Repeat with the remaining chops.

Place a wide, heavy-bottom saucepan over high heat. Add the butter and then the meat rolls and brown them quickly on all sides. Add the marsala and reduce the heat to a simmer. Cover and cook for about 10–15 minutes, until the meat is cooked through. Remove the rolls and keep them warm, and increase the heat to reduce the liquid for 2 minutes to thicken.

Serve the rolls on warmed plates with sautéed potatoes and a green salad and pour over a little of the sauce.

Ingredients

Serves 4

4 pork chops, bones and fat removed

4 large, thin slices Parma ham or San Daniele ham

4 large sage leaves

scant ½ cup unsalted butter

generous ¾ cup marsala, Madeira, or dry white wine

salt and pepper

sautéed potatoes and a green salad, to serve

WHOLE ARTICHOKES
WITH LEMON & THYME BUTTER

Ingredients

Serves 4

2 lemons

4 large globe artichokes

2 cups plus 2 tbsp butter

2 tbsp fresh thyme leaves

zest and juice of 1 lemon

salt and pepper

crusty bread, to serve

Method

Fill a large saucepan halfway with cold water. Halve the lemons, squeeze the juice into the water, and drop the skins in, too. Cut the stalks off the artichokes near the bottom, then "scalp" them by chopping off the top 1 inch/2.5 cm of the leaves. Add them to the water, cover, and bring to a boil. Once boiling, the artichokes will take 20–30 minutes to cook, depending on their tenderness and size. They are ready when the outer leaves can be pulled off without any effort.

Drain the artichokes, turn them upside down, and let cool for 15 minutes while you make your lemon and thyme butter. Gently melt the butter in a small saucepan, and mix in the thyme, lemon zest and juice, and salt and pepper.

Place the artichokes in a shallow bowl and season with salt and pepper. Pour the butter into small bowls—either individually or to share. Put a large bowl in the middle of the table for discarded artichoke parts and leaves. Serve with bread for mopping up.

RISOTTO PRIMAVERA

Method

Prepare the green vegetables: chop the asparagus into bite-size portions, cut the zucchini diagonally into finger-thick slices and trim the beans.

Bring a large saucepan of lightly salted water to a boil, add the green vegetables including the peas, and blanch for 1 minute, then remove and drain.

Place a large heavy-bottom saucepan over medium heat, add the olive oil and onions, and cook them gently for about 10 minutes, until softened. Add the rice and fry, stirring it into the oil for 2 minutes. Reduce the heat, add a ladleful of stock, and stir it into the rice as it absorbs. Gradually add more stock as each ladleful is absorbed. Check the rice—it should be slightly hard in the middle (you may need a little more or less of the liquid). Add the last ladle of stock, the Vermouth, and the herbs, and cook for an additional 5 minutes.

Add the butter, cheese, and blanched vegetables, check the seasoning, and heat through, stirring gently.

Serve in warmed bowls, with Parmesan cheese to sprinkle on top.

Ingredients

Serves 4

7 oz/200 g asparagus

1 zucchini

7 oz/200 g green beans

1¾ cups shelled fresh or frozen peas

2 tbsp olive oil

1 large onion, finely chopped

generous 1 cup arborio or other short-grain risotto rice

scant 3 cups warm chicken stock

3½ tbsp Vermouth or white wine

handful chopped parsley

1 tbsp fresh thyme leaves

5 tbsp butter

1¼ cups grated Parmesan cheese, plus extra to serve

salt and pepper

LINGUINI with CLAMS

Method

Cook the linguini according to the package instructions, drain, and toss with a splash of olive oil. Cover and keep warm.

Add half the olive oil to a large saucepan with a lid and place over high heat. Add the garlic, shallots, and chile and cook gently for 8–10 minutes, until softened. Add the wine, bring to a boil, and cook for 2 minutes. Add the clams, cover, and cook for an additional 2–5 minutes, or until all the clams have opened—discard any that haven't. Add the drained linguini, parsley, lemon zest, the remaining olive oil, and some salt and pepper and mix through.

Serve in warmed bowls, with another bowl for discarded shells.

Ingredients

Serves 2–4

7 oz/200 g dried linguini pasta

3 tbsp extra virgin olive oil

4 garlic cloves, finely chopped

2 shallots, finely chopped

½ fresh red chile, finely chopped

½ cup white wine

2 lb 4 oz/1 kg fresh clams, cleaned

handful of parsley, chopped

zest of 1 lemon

salt and pepper

ZABAGLIONE

Ingredients

Serves 6

⅓ cup superfine sugar

6 egg yolks

¾ cup marsala, Madeira, or other sweet dessert wine

splash of brandy

amaretti cookies, to serve

Method

Fill a saucepan halfway with water and bring to a boil. Place a heatproof bowl over the pan so that it doesn't quite touch the boiling water.

Put the sugar and eggs into the bowl and whisk until light and creamy. Add the marsala a little at a time, whisking continuously, then add the brandy and continue whisking for up to 15 minutes, until you have a floaty, silky foam.

Pour it into bowls and serve with amaretti cookies. It can also be made ahead of time and served chilled.

PANETTONE BREAD-AND-BUTTER PUDDING

Ingredients

Serves 4–6

scant 1 cup raisins, golden raisins, or chopped dates

4 tbsp brandy

1¼ cups milk

scant 2 cups heavy cream

1 vanilla bean, split, or 1 tsp vanilla extract

scant ¾ cup butter, softened, plus extra for greasing

10 medium loaf-size slices of panettone, preferably chocolate-flavored, or white bread, crusts removed

4 eggs

¾ cup superfine sugar

vanilla ice cream, to serve

Method

Put the raisins in a bowl with the brandy and let soften for an hour or two. In a small saucepan, warm (but don't boil) the milk and cream and add the split vanilla bean. Let stand for 30 minutes.

Preheat the oven to 350°F/180°C. Butter a shallow ovenproof bowl. Butter the panettone slices, cut them diagonally in half, and lay in an overlapping pattern in the bowl. Remove the softened raisins from the brandy, reserving the brandy, and sprinkle them over the panettone.

In a large bowl, whisk the eggs with the sugar. Remove the vanilla bean from the milk and discard, and add the cream and milk to the egg mixture. Add the reserved brandy and whisk. Pour this mixture over the panettone and press the slices down so that they soak in the custard. Make sure that the edges don't stick out too far above the surface of the custard.

Transfer to the preheated oven and bake for 30–40 minutes, until the custard has dried and set golden brown but before the panettone burns. Serve hot, with vanilla ice cream.

RICH ITALIAN CHOCOLATE CAKE

Method

Preheat the oven to 350°F/180°C. Grease a 10-inch/25-cm round springform cake pan with butter and sprinkle with flour. Shake the flour around the whole of the inside of the pan so that all the butter is covered, then knock out the excess flour.

Place the hazelnuts on a baking sheet and bake in the preheated oven for 5 minutes, then let cool. While the nuts are baking, chop the chocolate into small pieces and place in a food processor with the almonds. Blend on and off until the mixture is the consistency of breadcrumbs.

Transfer the mixture to a large metal bowl and stir in the brandy, coffee, cinnamon, milk, and half the superfine sugar. Add the egg yolks, one at a time, and continue to mix, blending well. Place the roasted hazelnuts in a clean dish towel and rub vigorously to remove the skins. Add the

nuts to the food processor. Blend on and off, until the nuts are slightly coarser than the almonds and chocolate. Add to the mixture and combine well.

In a clean bowl, whisk the egg whites until stiff, add the remaining superfine sugar, and continue to whisk until shiny. Fold the egg whites into the mixture with a large metal spoon, a few spoonfuls at a time, with a cutting movement of the spoon so that you don't knock too much air out of the egg whites.

Gently spoon the mixture into the prepared cake pan, and bake in the center of the oven for an hour. The cake is ready when a skewer inserted into the center comes out dry.

Unclip the cake, turn out onto a wire rack, and let cool. Serve with some mascarpone cheese.

Ingredients

Serves 6

butter, for greasing

flour, for dusting

2 cups hazelnuts

225 g/8 oz semisweet chocolate

2 cups blanched almonds

5 tbsp brandy

2 tbsp espresso coffee

1 tsp ground cinnamon

2 tbsp milk

generous 1 cup superfine sugar

5 large eggs, separated, at room temperature

mascarpone cheese, to serve

BARCELONA

It is often said that most people in the world eat to live, but Spaniards live to eat. And nowhere is this more evident than in Barcelona—the Catalonian capital where the Pyrenees meet the Mediterranean—with its thriving tapas culture and popular restaurants. Food in the city tends to be flavorsome and traditional, rather than trendy or making concessions to passing fads, and expensive and simple meals alike begin with Tomato-Rubbed Bread. The best produce and other ingredients the city has to offer are on display at La Boqueria, the famed nineteenth-century market. This vast metal and glass structure is a must-see on any visit, and the restaurants that surround the perimeter provide an inexpensive, authentic sampling of the city's cooking.

BABY FAVA BEANS & CHORIZO

Ingredients

Serves 4

1 tbsp olive oil

9 oz/250 g fresh chorizo sausage, chopped into finger-thick circles.

4 scallions, sliced

3 garlic cloves, crushed

generous ⅓ cup chicken stock or vegetable stock, warmed

4 lb 8 oz/2 kg young fava beans in their pods, or about 1 lb 10 oz/750 g shelled frozen baby fava beans

1 large handful fresh mint, chopped

salt and pepper

toasted sourdough bread, to serve

Method

Place a heavy-bottom skillet over medium heat and add the olive oil. When it's shimmering hot, add the chorizo and brown it on all sides for about 15 minutes. Remove it from the skillet and set aside. Reduce the heat, add the scallions and garlic, and fry for an additional 5 minutes. Add the stock and fava beans and simmer for about 3–5 minutes, until the beans are just tender. Add the mint and the cooked chorizo, stir through, and season with salt and pepper. Serve, with the juices, on small warmed plates, with some sourdough toast on the side.

TOMATO-RUBBED BREAD

Method

If the bread is soft, toast it under a preheated broiler until lightly golden on both sides. Rub each slice of bread with half a fresh juicy tomato. If using, sprinkle over the chopped garlic and drizzle the olive oil over the top.

Ingredients

Serves 4 as part of a tapas meal

4 slices French bread

2 ripe tomatoes, halved

1 garlic clove, finely chopped (optional)

2 tbsp Spanish olive oil (optional)

GAZPACHO

Ingredients

Serves 4

1 red bell pepper, cored, seeded, and chopped

2 lb 4 oz/1 kg ripe tomatoes, cored and chopped

2 tbsp very finely chopped onion

3 garlic cloves, crushed

1 cucumber, peeled and chopped

3½ slices stale bread, crumbled

3 tbsp red wine vinegar or sherry vinegar

3½ tbsp olive oil, plus extra for drizzling

ice cubes (optional)

salt and pepper

Method

Set aside a handful of the red bell pepper, a handful of the tomatoes, and half the chopped onion in the refrigerator. Put the rest in a food processor with the garlic, and cucumber, and puree until smooth. Add the bread, vinegar, and oil and blend again. Season with salt and pepper to taste. If the soup is too thick, add some ice, then place in the refrigerator for 2 hours.

When ready to serve, check the vinegar and seasoning and ladle into bowls. Scatter over the reserved red bell pepper, tomatoes, and onions, then drizzle over a swirl of olive oil. Serve.

FIDEUÀ

Method

To make the sofregit, put the onion and oil in a 10-in/25-cm paella pan or heavy-bottom skillet with a tight-fitting lid and place over medium heat. Cook, stirring occasionally, for 10 minutes, or until the onions are softened and just starting to color. Reduce the heat to very low and continue cooking for an additional 10–20 minutes, until they are golden brown. Add the tomatoes and their juices and the chile, increase the heat, and continue to simmer, stirring, for 15 minutes, or until the tomatoes are reduced to a pulp and start to give off the oil they have absorbed.

Meanwhile, put the stock in a saucepan with the reserved shrimp shells and simmer over low heat for 10 minutes. Strain, discard the shells, then return the liquid to the pan with the saffron and ½ teaspoon salt and bring to a boil. Turn off the heat, cover the pan, and set aside.

Wipe out the sofregit pan. Add the oil to the pan and heat over medium heat. Add the noodles and fry for 10 minutes, stirring continuously, until they are golden brown and look "cooked." Stir the sofregit into the noodles, then add the stock and bring to a boil, stirring with a long-handled wooden spoon: the mixture will spatter when the sofregit is added. Reduce the heat to medium and stir for 8–10 minutes, until all the liquid is absorbed and the noodles are tender. Adjust the seasoning to taste.

Discard any open mussels or clams that do not close when tapped. Arrange the shrimp, mussels, clams, and squid on top of the noodles, reduce the heat to very low, cover the pan tightly, and let steam for 5 minutes, or until the shrimp are pink, the mussels and clams are open, and the squid turn white and lose their translucency.

Discard any closed mussels or clams. Adjust the seasoning to taste. Serve immediately with lemon wedges for squeezing over each portion and a bowl of aïoli on the side.

Ingredients

Serves 4–6

scant 3 cups fish stock

12 jumbo shrimp, peeled, heads removed, tails left on, shells reserved

large pinch saffron threads

2 tbsp olive oil

1 lb 2 oz/500 g thin, hollow Spanish noodles (fidos, or fideu in Catalan), or angel hair pasta, broken into small pieces

12 large mussels, scrubbed and debearded

12 clams, scrubbed

6 small cleaned squid bodies with tentacles

salt and pepper

lemon wedges and aïoli, to serve

SOFREGIT

1 onion, chopped

3½ tbsp garlic-flavored olive oil

2 large tomatoes, grated, skins and cores discarded

1 fresh red chile, seeded and thinly sliced

TRADITIONAL CATALAN SALT COD SALAD

Method

Place the dried salt cod in a large bowl, cover with cold water, and let soak for at least 48 hours, changing the water occasionally.

Pat the salt cod dry with paper towels and remove the skin and bones, then use your fingers to tear into fine shreds. Put in a large, nonmetallic bowl with the scallions, oil, vinegar, and lemon juice, and toss together. Season with freshly ground black pepper, cover, and put in the refrigerator to marinate for 3 hours.

Stir in the bell peppers and olives. Taste and adjust the seasoning, if necessary, remembering that the cod and olives might be salty. Arrange the tomato slices on a large platter or individual plates and spoon the salad on top. Sprinkle with parsley and serve.

Ingredients

Serves 4–6

14 oz/400 g dried salt cod in one piece

6 scallions, sliced thinly on the diagonal

6 tbsp extra virgin olive oil

1 tbsp sherry vinegar

1 tbsp lemon juice

2 large red bell peppers, broiled, peeled, seeded, and diced very finely

12 large black olives, pitted and sliced

pepper

2 large, juicy tomatoes, sliced thinly, to serve

2 tbsp very finely chopped fresh parsley, to garnish

CHICKEN AND HAM CROQUETTES

Ingredients

Serves 4

4 tbsp Spanish olive oil or butter

4 tbsp all-purpose flour

¾ cup milk

1 cup ground, cooked chicken

2 oz/55 g Serrano or cooked ham, very finely chopped

1 tbsp chopped fresh flat-leaf parsley

small pinch of freshly grated nutmeg

1 egg, beaten

1 cup day-old white breadcrumbs

corn oil, for deep-frying

salt and pepper

aïoli, for dipping

Method

Heat the olive oil or butter in a pan. Stir in the flour to form a paste and cook gently for 1 minute, stirring constantly. Remove the pan from the heat and gradually stir in the milk until smooth. Return to the heat and slowly bring to a boil, stirring constantly, until the mixture thickens.

Remove the pan from the heat, add the ground chicken, and beat until the mixture is smooth. Add the chopped ham, parsley, and nutmeg and mix well. Season the mixture to taste with salt and pepper. Spread the chicken mixture in a dish and let stand for 30 minutes until cool, then cover and let chill for 2–3 hours or overnight. Don't be tempted to skip this stage, as chilling the croquettes helps to stop them falling apart when they are cooked.

When the chicken mixture has chilled, pour the beaten egg onto a plate and spread the breadcrumbs out on a separate plate. Divide the chicken mixture into 8 equal-size portions. With dampened hands, form each portion into a cylindrical shape. Dip the croquettes, one at a time, in the beaten egg, then roll in the breadcrumbs to coat them. Place on a plate and let chill for 1 hour.

To cook, heat the corn oil in a deep-fat fryer to 350–375°F/180–190°C, or until a cube of bread browns in 30 seconds. Add the croquettes, in batches to prevent the temperature of the oil from dropping, and deep-fry for 5–10 minutes, or until golden brown and crispy. Remove with a slotted spoon and drain well on paper towels.

Serve the chicken and ham croquettes piping hot, accompanied by a bowl of aïoli for dipping.

CATALAN PORK STEW

Ingredients

Serves 4–6

olive oil, for browning

4 lb 8 oz/2 kg boneless pork shoulder, cut into 3-inch/7.5-cm chunks and patted dry

bouquet garni of parsley, thyme, and a bay leaf, tied with string

3 cups white Catalan wine, such as Chenin Blanc

3 cups peeled carrots, cut into ½-inch/1-cm slices

1 lb 2 oz/800 g canned chickpeas, drained and rinsed

salt and pepper

SOFREGIT

2 onions, chopped

½ cup olive oil

4 large tomatoes, grated, skins and cores discarded

4 large garlic cloves, finely chopped

1 tbsp hot Spanish paprika

PICADA

1 slice day-old country bread, fried in olive oil

1 tbsp blanched almonds, toasted

1 tbsp skinned hazelnuts, toasted

2 garlic cloves, crushed

1 oz/30 g bittersweet Spanish chocolate

olive oil, as required

Method

To make the sofregit, put the onions and oil in a large flameproof casserole and place over a medium–high heat. Cook, stirring occasionally, for 10 minutes. Reduce the heat to very low and continue cooking for another 10–20 minutes, until the onions are golden brown. Add the tomatoes and their juices, garlic, and paprika, increase the heat, and continue to simmer, stirring, for 15 minutes, or until the tomatoes are reduced to a pulp and start to give off the oil they have absorbed.

Preheat the oven to 325°F/160°C. Pour a thin layer of oil into a casserole and heat over medium–high heat. Add the pork and brown on all sides in batches, adding more oil if necessary. Pour off any excess fat. Return the pork to the pan. Stir in the sofregit, herbs, and salt and pepper to taste. Pour in the wine and enough water to cover all the meat, then bring to a boil. Cover and place in the preheated oven. After 1¼ hours stir in the carrots, re-cover the pan, and return it to the oven for 30 minutes, or until the pork and carrots are tender.

Meanwhile, to make the picada, tear the bread into a food processor, then add the almonds, hazelnuts, garlic, and chocolate and whiz until finely blended. With the motor running, slowly pour in enough olive oil to form a thick paste.

Transfer the casserole to the stovetop. Remove the pork and carrots and set aside. Bring the cooking liquid to a boil and place several ladlefuls in a heatproof bowl. Stir in the picada until well blended, then stir this mixture into the cooking liquid and continue boiling for 2 minutes. Reduce the heat and add the pork, carrots, and chickpeas. Simmer for about 5 minutes, or until the stew thickens and the chickpeas are hot. Adjust the seasoning, if necessary, and serve.

FLAM

Ingredients
Makes 5

scant 2½ cups whole milk

½ orange with 2 long, thin pieces of rind removed

1 vanilla bean, split, or ½ tsp vanilla extract

scant 1 cup superfine sugar

butter, for greasing the dish

3 large eggs, plus 2 large egg yolks

Method

Pour the milk into a pan with the orange rind and vanilla bean or extract. Bring to a boil, then remove from the heat and stir in ½ cup of the sugar; set aside for at least 30 minutes to steep.

Meanwhile, put the remaining sugar and 4 tablespoons of water in another pan over medium–high heat. Stir until the sugar dissolves, then boil without stirring until the caramel turns deep golden brown.

Immediately remove the pan from the heat and squeeze in a few drops of orange juice to stop the cooking. Pour into a lightly buttered 5-cup soufflé dish and swirl to cover the bottom; set aside.

When the milk has steeped, return the pan to the heat, and bring the milk to a simmer. Beat the whole eggs and egg yolks together in a heatproof bowl. Pour the warm milk into the eggs, whisking constantly. Strain this mixture into the soufflé dish.

Place the soufflé dish in a roasting pan and pour in enough boiling water to come halfway up the sides of the dish. Bake in a preheated oven, 325°F/160°C, for 75–90 minutes, until set and a knife inserted in the center comes out clean.

Remove the soufflé dish from the roasting pan and set aside to cool completely. Cover and let chill overnight.

To serve, run a metal spatula round the side of the dish, then invert onto a serving plate with a rim, shaking firmly to release.

CHOCOLATE HAZELNUT CAKE

Method

Put one third of the hazelnuts in a blender and pulse until very finely ground, then set aside. Preheat the oven to 350°F/180°C and line the bottom of a 9-inch/23-cm round cake pan with wax paper.

Put the butter and chocolate in a heatproof bowl set over a saucepan of gently simmering water and heat until melted. Set aside to cool. Beat the eggs, sugar, and vanilla extract together for 3 minutes, until light and fluffy. Stir in the chocolate and butter. Sift over the flour, baking powder, salt, and ground hazelnuts, rubbing the hazelnuts through the sifter with a wooden spoon. Toss the raisins and whole hazelnuts with 1 tablespoon of flour, then fold them into the batter.

Pour the batter into the prepared pan and smooth the surface. Bake for 45 minutes, or until a toothpick inserted in the center comes out clean and the cake comes away from the side of the pan. Let cool in the pan for 10 minutes, then turn out, remove the paper, and let cool on a wire rack. Transfer to a plate and sift over some confectioners' sugar.

Ingredients

Serves 6

scant 1 cup skinned hazelnuts, lightly toasted

¾ cup butter, softened, plus extra for greasing

3 oz/85 g bittersweet Spanish chocolate (at least 85% cocoa solids)

4 extra-large eggs, beaten

½ cup sugar

1 tsp vanilla extract

⅓ cup all-purpose flour, plus 1 tbsp extra

½ tsp baking powder

pinch of salt

scant 1 cup raisins, soaked in 2 tbsp Spanish brandy

confectioners' sugar, to decorate

GOAT CHEESE WITH HONEY & WALNUTS

Ingredients

Serves 4

about 6 oz/175 g goat cheese, such as Monte Enebro, in one piece

about ⅓ cup clear honey, such as orange-blossom or thyme-flavored

⅔ cup walnut halves, chopped

Method

Remove the cheese from the refrigerator at least 20 minutes before serving to let it come to room temperature.

Pour the honey into a bowl. Place the walnuts in another bowl.

Serve the cheese on a board with a cheese knife and let everyone cut a slice for themselves. They then drizzle some honey over, with a dipper, if available, and sprinkle with chopped walnuts.

Alternatively, cut the cheese into 4 slices and place a slice on each of 4 serving plates. Drizzle some honey over, sprinkle with chopped nuts, and serve.

BERLIN

Meat reigns supreme in Berlin, but there is more to the city's
food culture than just sausages, sauerkraut, and beer. Meals
are filling and traditional. Pork, potatoes, and apples feature
in many hearty, savory dishes, yet pastry chefs also make
their marks with traditional Stollen, a Christmas favorite,
and Poppy Seed Cake, often enjoyed with a cup of strong
coffee. The meat-and-fruit combination is especially popular
in classics, such as Fried Calf's Liver with Apples & Onions,
a filling meal easily complemented by one of the local beers.
For many Berliners, a meal simply isn't complete without
potatoes in one form or another—Berlin Meatballs with
Potato Salad, and Potato Soup are popular examples.

BERLIN MEATBALLS & POTATO SALAD

Ingredients

Serves 3–4

2 thick slices day-old white bread, crusts removed

1 cup warm milk

9 oz/250 g lean ground beef

9 oz/250 g lean ground pork

1 large egg, lightly beaten

1 tbsp chopped fresh parsley

salt and freshly ground white pepper

freshly grated nutmeg

curry powder

4 tbsp butter

1 large onion, sliced thinly into rings

salad

1 lb 8 oz/750 g waxy new potatoes, scraped, or firm-textured old potatoes, scrubbed

2–3 tbsp hot veal or beef stock

1 tbsp vinegar

½ cup chopped onion

1 tsp butter

4 tbsp diced bacon

1 tsp cornstarch

scant tsp brown sugar

2 tbsp water

2 tbsp sour cream

1 tbsp finely chopped fresh chives

1 tbsp finely chopped fresh parsley

salt and pepper

Method

Place the bread in a bowl, pour over the milk, and let soak for 10 minutes. Place the ground beef and pork in a bowl and mix together well. Squeeze any excess milk out of the bread and add the bread to the meat in the bowl. Add the beaten egg and the parsley, then add salt and pepper, nutmeg, and curry powder to taste. Shape the meat mixture into balls and flatten them slightly. Heat the butter in a heavy-bottom skillet over medium–low heat and fry the meatballs, turning once, for 5–7 minutes, or until browned all over and cooked through. Transfer to a warmed serving dish. Add the onion rings to the pan and fry until crispy and lightly browned.

To make the salad, steam the new potatoes, for 15–20 minutes, until tender. Slice the cooked potatoes into a warm dish, gently stir in enough hot stock to coat, and set aside to keep warm. Mix the onion and vinegar together. Melt the butter in a small pan over medium heat and cook the bacon for 2 minutes. Mix together the cornstarch, sugar, and water and add to the pan with the onion-and-vinegar mixture. Cook, stirring, for 2–3 minutes, until the mixture clears and thickens. Remove from the heat and stir in the sour cream and herbs. Season to taste with salt and pepper.

Serve the potato salad with the meatballs and onion rings piled on top.

POTATO SOUP

Ingredients

Serves 4

3 tbsp butter

1 medium onion, peeled and chopped

1 leek, tough outer leaves removed, sliced

1 large carrot, peeled and chopped

1 small parsnip, peeled and chopped

1 small celeriac, peeled and chopped

1 celery stalk, chopped

1 parsley root, peeled and finely diced

1 sprig of fresh parsley

1 lb/450 g starchy potatoes, cut into chunks

3 tbsp flour

5 cups water

2 tsp dried marjoram

salt and pepper

2 tbsp each finely chopped fresh parsley and dill, to garnish

Method

Melt the butter in a large, heavy-bottom saucepan, add the onion, leek, carrot, parsnip, celeriac, celery stalk, parsley root, and parsley sprig and cook over medium heat, stirring constantly, for 7–8 minutes, or until the vegetables are soft and golden.

Add the potatoes and cook, stirring, for another 4–5 minutes, or until the potatoes start to color. Stir in the flour and cook until it starts to brown.

Pour over the water, stir in the marjoram, season to taste with salt and pepper, and bring to a boil. Reduce the heat and simmer for 30 minutes, or until the potatoes are tender.

Transfer the soup to a food processor and process until smooth. Return to the pan and heat through, then serve garnished with chopped parsley and dill.

POTATO FRITTERS

Ingredients

Serves 4–5

2 lb 4 oz/1 kg starchy potatoes, peeled

1 large egg

2 tbsp flour

vegetable oil, for frying

sugar, for dusting

salt

apple sauce, to serve

Method

Coarsely grate the potatoes into a bowl of water to prevent discoloration, then drain them and dry thoroughly on a clean dish towel. Transfer to a bowl, then add the egg, salt to taste, and flour, and mix thoroughly.

Pour vegetable oil into a large, heavy-bottom skillet to a depth of ½ inch/1 cm and place over medium–high heat. When the oil is hot, drop in large spoonfuls of the potato mixture, in batches of 3 or 4, set well apart. Flatten each fritter with a palette knife and fry, turning once, until golden brown on both sides. Remove from the pan and drain on paper towels, then keep warm while you cook the remaining fritters. Serve warm with apple sauce.

FRIED CALF'S LIVER WITH APPLES & ONIONS

Method

Melt 1 tablespoon of butter in a skillet over medium–low heat and fry the apple slices on both sides until just soft. Remove carefully from the pan with a spatula and keep warm.

Add the onion slices to the pan and fry until golden, adding a little more butter if necessary.

Meanwhile, melt the remaining butter over low heat in another skillet. Dust the liver slices lightly with flour and fry very gently for about 4 minutes, turning frequently, until golden brown all over on the outside but still pink inside.

Remove from the heat and season with salt, white pepper, and nutmeg to taste. Serve with the apple and onion slices on top, accompanied with red cabbage and mashed potato.

Ingredients

Serves 4

about 4 tbsp butter

2 green apples, peeled, cored, and sliced

2 medium onions, peeled and sliced into rings

1 lb/450 g calf's liver, cut into ¼-inch/5 mm slices

1 tbsp flour

salt and freshly ground white pepper

freshly grated nutmeg

red cabbage and mashed potato, to serve

MEATBALLS IN LEMON-CAPER SAUCE

Method

Place the bread in a small bowl, cover with the water, and soak for 10 minutes, then squeeze out any excess water. Place the soaked bread in a large mixing bowl and add the ground beef and veal or pork, marjoram, egg yolks, and salt and pepper to taste.

Melt the butter in a saucepan and fry the onion until lightly colored. Add it to the meat mixture with the lemon rind and anchovies and mix well. Form the mixture into small balls.

Bring the stock to a boil in a large, heavy-bottom saucepan, add the meatballs, then reduce the heat to medium–low and simmer for about 20 minutes, or until the meatballs rise to the surface. Remove with a slotted spoon and keep warm. Reserve the stock.

To make the sauce, melt the butter in a large saucepan over medium heat. Whisk in the flour and cook for 1 minute, still whisking, then gradually whisk in the reserved stock. Add the capers and lemon juice and season to taste. Add the meatballs and heat through for 5 minutes. Mix the egg yolks into the sour cream and stir into the meatballs and sauce. Heat gently to thicken the sauce, then serve the meatballs on a bed of egg noodles, sprinkled with extra freshly ground black pepper.

Ingredients

Serves 4

2 thick slices day-old white bread, crusts removed

generous 1 cup cold water

9 oz/250 g lean ground beef

9 oz/250 g lean ground veal or pork

1½ tsp chopped fresh marjoram or ½ tsp dried marjoram

2 medium egg yolks

1 tbsp butter

1 medium onion, grated

finely grated rind of ½ lemon

3 anchovy fillets, finely chopped

3 cups chicken stock

freshly cooked egg noodles, to serve

salt and pepper

sauce

2 tbsp butter

2 tbsp flour

2 tbsp capers, chopped

1 tbsp lemon juice

2 medium egg yolks

⅔ cup sour cream

HAM HOCKS WITH SAUERKRAUT

Ingredients

Serves 6

6 ham hocks, cleaned, split, and rinsed under cold running water

1 onion, peeled and left whole

2 bay leaves

1 tbsp pickling spice

8 black peppercorns, lightly crushed

salt

sauerkraut, to serve

fresh parsley, finely chopped, to garnish

Method

Place the ham hocks in a large, heavy-bottom saucepan and pour over water to cover. Add the onion, bay leaves, pickling spice, and peppercorns and season to taste with salt. Cover the pan, bring to a boil, reduce the heat, and simmer over medium–low heat for about 3 hours, or until the meat is tender but still clinging to the bone. Remove the hocks from the pan and drain well.

Divide the ham hocks between individual plates and serve with sauerkraut, garnished with fresh parsley.

SAUERBRAUTEN WITH RED CABBAGE

Ingredients

Serves 8

4 lb/1.8 kg boneless beef joint

2 tbsp lard or vegetable oil

1 onion, chopped

4 carrots, chopped

2 celery stalks, chopped

2 tbsp all-purpose flour

generous ⅓ cup water

1 cup crumbled gingersnaps

salt and pepper

boiled potatoes and red cabbage, to serve

marinade

1½ cups red wine

generous 1 cup red wine vinegar

1 cup water

2 onions, quartered

2 tsp black peppercorns, lightly crushed

2 tsp juniper berries, lightly crushed

4 bay leaves

2 cloves

1 tbsp salt

2 tbsp sugar

Method

Place all the marinade ingredients in a nonmetallic bowl large enough to hold the meat and stir until the sugar and salt dissolve. Add the meat, cover, and place in a cool place for 3 days. Turn the meat in the marinade each morning and evening.

Preheat the oven to 325°F/170°C. Remove the meat from the marinade and pat dry with paper towels. Season with salt and pepper. Strain the marinade and discard the spices and onions. Place a large flameproof casserole dish over a high heat and add the lard. When hot, add the beef and brown it quickly on all sides. Remove it and reserve. Reduce the heat a little, add the vegetables, and fry for 5 minutes. Add the flour, stir, and cook for an additional 2 minutes. Add 2¼ cups of the marinade and the water.

Cover the casserole tightly, place in the preheated oven, and cook for 2½ hours, checking after 1½ hours to make sure it isn't drying out. If it is, add more marinade.

Remove the meat from the casserole, cover, and keep warm while you make the sauce. Strain the remaining cooking liquid from the casserole into a saucepan and add the marinade to make it up to about 2¼ cups. Add the crumbled cookies and simmer for 15 minutes, until it thickens. Season to taste.

Carve the meat and serve with the sauce, boiled potatoes, and red cabbage.

POPPY SEED CAKE

Ingredients

Serves 4

pastry

10 tbsp butter, at room temperature

generous 3 tbsp superfine sugar

pinch of salt

1 large egg

scant 1½ cups all-purpose flour

filling

1¼ cups poppy seeds, ground, plus 1 tbsp whole poppy seeds

6 tbsp milk

generous ½ cup granulated sugar

¼ cup grated semisweet chocolate

⅓ cup raisins

¾ cup candied peel, chopped

⅓ cup blanched almonds, grated

1 large egg, beaten

1 tbsp superfine sugar

Method

To make the pastry, beat together the butter, sugar and salt, add the egg, then stir in the flour and just enough cold water to make a soft dough. Cover in plastic wrap and chill in the refrigerator for 1 hour.

Meanwhile, to make the filling, place the ground poppy seeds and milk in a saucepan and simmer, stirring, for 2 minutes. Remove the pan from the heat and stir in the granulated sugar, chocolate, raisins, candied peel, and almonds. Set aside 1 teaspoon of the beaten egg and beat the remainder into the mixture.

Roll the pastry out thinly on a lightly floured counter and cut four 8-inch/20-cm circles. Place one circle in a 8-inch/20-cm loose-bottom tart pan and spread over one third of the filling. Repeat the layers, finishing with the last pastry circle. Press the edges together very lightly, then make a hole in the center with the handle of a wooden spoon.

Brush the cake with the reserved beaten egg, then sprinkle with the superfine sugar and whole poppy seeds. Bake in a preheated oven, 325°F/160°C, for about 45 minutes, until golden. Serve warm or cold.

BAKED APPLES WITH VANILLA SAUCE

Ingredients

Serves 4

4 large cooking apples, washed and dried

2 oz/55 g marzipan

about 1 tbsp rum

2 tbsp golden raisins

2 tbsp butter

1¼ cups dry white wine

4 tbsp apricot jam

vanilla sauce

2 cups milk

½ vanilla bean

3 egg yolks

¼ cup sugar

2 tsp cornstarch

Method

Core the apples most of the way through from the stalk end, then score lightly around the middle with a sharp knife. Using a fork, soften the marzipan with the rum, then work in the raisins. Place a little butter in each apple, then divide the marzipan filling between them and top with a little more butter.

Preheat the oven to 375°F/190°C. Place the apples in a ovenproof bowl and pour in the wine. Bake for 25–30 minutes, basting occasionally with the wine. Transfer to a serving dish. Strain the wine into a saucepan, stir in the apricot jam, and simmer, stirring, until reduced to a thick syrup. Spoon over the apples and cool for 1 hour.

To make the vanilla sauce, bring the milk and vanilla to scalding point in a heatproof bowl set over a saucepan of simmering water. Beat the egg yolks, sugar, and cornstarch in a large, heatproof bowl until light and frothy. Gradually add the milk, stirring constantly. Set over the pan of simmering water and cook, stirring, until the sauce thickens. Remove the vanilla bean and serve the sauce with the apples.

STOLLEN

Ingredients

Serves 8

⅔ cup lukewarm milk

¼ cup superfine sugar

2 tsp active dry yeast

2½ cups white bread flour

½ tsp salt

½ cup butter, softened, plus extra for greasing

1 medium egg, beaten

¼ cup currants

⅓ cup golden raisins

55 g/2 oz candied peel, finely diced

¼ cup candied cherries

3 tbsp chopped, blanched almonds

grated rind of ½ lemon

6 oz/175 g marzipan, formed into a 9-inch/23-cm sausage

1 cup confectioners' sugar, sifted

1 tbsp water

Method

Pour the warm milk into a small bowl, add 1 teaspoon of the sugar, sprinkle over the yeast, and whisk thoroughly. Set aside for 10 minutes, until a frothy head has formed.

Set aside 2 tablespoons of flour and sift the rest into a large mixing bowl with the salt and remaining sugar. Make a well in the center, pour in the yeast mixture, then add the butter and beaten egg. Mix well to form a soft dough.

Work in the currants, raisins, peel, cherries, almonds, and lemon rind, then transfer the dough to a counter and knead for 5 minutes, until smooth and elastic. Place in a clean bowl, cover with plastic wrap and let stand in a warm place for 1½–2 hours, until doubled in size.

Sprinkle the reserved flour onto a counter and turn out the dough onto it. Punch out the air, then knead again until smooth and elastic. Roll out to a 10 x 8-inch/25 x 20-cm rectangle and place the marzipan in the center.

Fold the dough over the marzipan and place, seam-side down, on a greased baking sheet. Cover and set aside until doubled in size, then bake in a preheated oven, 375°F/190°C, for 35–40 minutes, until risen and golden. Transfer to a wire rack to cool a little.

Mix the confectioners' sugar with the water and spread it thinly over the stollen while it is still warm. Serve cut into slices.

NEW DELHI

Food in Delhi is as exciting and varied as India's capital city itself. Spiced street food and snacks, or chaats, are an integral part of city life, sometimes eaten outdoors on the go or as part of an indoor meal. Luxury hotels serve refined international cuisine for the wealthy and tourists, but it is the everyday food from thousands of stalls in markets and bazaars and on street corners that capture the spirit of India, with the dynamic mix of religions that so strongly influence the eating habits of millions. Lamb Burra, Whole Tandoori Chicken, and Salt Lassis are just some of the recipes that make it easy to savor an authentic flavor of India at home. With a large resident vegetarian population, visiting vegetarians have more choices here than in many other cities, with restaurants always offering nonmeat options.

TARKA DHAL

Ingredients

Serves 4

1 cup red lentils

3½ cups water

1 tsp salt, or to taste

2 tsp sunflower or olive oil

½ tsp black or brown mustard seeds

½ tsp cumin seeds

4 shallots, finely chopped

2 green chiles, chopped (seeded if you like)

1 tsp ground turmeric

1 tsp ground cumin

1 fresh tomato, chopped

2 tbsp chopped fresh cilantro leaves

basmati rice or naan, to serve

Method

Wash the lentils until the water runs clear and put into a medium saucepan. Add the water and bring to a boil. Reduce the heat to medium and skim off the froth. Cook, uncovered, for 10 minutes. Reduce the heat to low, cover, and cook for 45 minutes, stirring occasionally to ensure that the lentils do not stick to the bottom of the pan as they thicken. Stir in the salt.

Meanwhile, heat the oil in a small saucepan over medium heat. When hot but not smoking, add the mustard seeds, followed by the cumin seeds. Add the shallots and chiles and cook, stirring, for 2–3 minutes, then add the turmeric and ground cumin. Add the tomato and cook, stirring, for 30 seconds.

Fold the shallot mixture into the cooked lentils. Stir in the cilantro, remove from the heat, and serve immediately with basmati rice or naan.

ALOO TIKA

Ingredients

Serves 4

2 large baking potatoes, about ½ lb/225 g
each

1 cup frozen peas

1 tsp garam masala

1 tsp salt

½ tsp turmeric

½ red onion, minced

½ fresh red chile, seeded and finely
chopped

sunflower oil or peanut oil, for oiling and
frying

⅓ cup chickpea flour, seasoned with salt
and pepper

pepper

selection of chutneys, relishes, and dips,
to serve

Method

Put the potatoes in a large saucepan of
water, bring to a boil, and cook for
15 minutes, or until just tender. Do not
overcook. Drain the potatoes and set aside
until cool enough to handle, then peel and
grate them into a large bowl.

Meanwhile, bring another saucepan of
lightly salted water to a boil, add the peas,
and cook for 5 minutes, or until tender.
Drain well and add to the bowl with the
potatoes. Add the garam masala, salt,
turmeric, and pepper to taste and use
your hands to mix. Add the onion
and chile and use your hands to work
everything together.

Wash and dry your hands, then lightly
grease them with the oil. Roll the potato
mixture into 16 equal balls, then flatten
them between your palms. Put the
chickpea flour on a plate. Pat the flour
onto both sides of the patties, shaking off
the excess.

Heat about ¼ inch/5 mm of the oil in a
large skillet over high heat. Fry the patties
in batches for 2 minutes on each side, or
until golden brown and crispy.

Serve warm, with a selection of chutneys,
relishes, and dips.

SAVORY CHEESECAKES

Ingredients

Makes 8

2 large slices one- or two-day-old white bread,
crusts removed

8 oz/225 g paneer, provolone cheese, or firm
tofu (drained weight), grated

3 shallots, finely chopped

1 tsp fennel seeds

½ tsp cumin seeds

1 tbsp chopped fresh mint leaves or ½ tsp dried
mint

2 tbsp chopped fresh cilantro leaves

1 tsp ginger paste

¼ cup slivered almonds, lightly crushed
(optional)

1 green chile, chopped (seeded if you like)

½ tsp garam masala

½ tsp chili powder (optional)

½ tsp salt, or to taste

1 tbsp lemon juice

1 large egg, beaten

sunflower or vegetable oil, for pan-frying

Method

Soak the bread slices in a bowl of water for
1–2 minutes, then squeeze out all the water and
crumble the slices between your palms. Put the
bread in a large bowl and add all the remaining
ingredients, except the oil. Mix well to form a
binding consistency.

Divide the mixture in half and shape each half into
4 equal-size, flat cakes ¼ inch/5 mm thick.

Pour oil into a skillet to a depth of 1 inch/2.5 cm
and heat over medium heat. Add the cakes and
cook for 5 minutes on each side, or until well
browned. Drain on paper towels and serve hot.

WHOLE TANDOORI CHICKEN

Method

Cut two slits into each chicken leg and two into each thigh. They should just reach the bone. Make two shallower cuts into the fleshiest part of each breast. These are to let the marinade penetrate into the meat.

Mix all the remaining ingredients together in a food processor and blend to a smooth paste. Place the chicken in a large, nonmetallic dish and cover it in the paste, massaging it deep into the skin and flesh. Place the chicken, uncovered, in the refrigerator to marinate for as long as possible—preferably 24 hours.

Remove the chicken from the refrigerator an hour before cooking to warm it to room temperature. Preheat the oven to 425°F/220°C. Place the chicken in the oven and cook, uncovered, for 20 minutes, then reduce the heat to 350°F/180°C. Baste the chicken and cook for an additional 35 minutes. Turn off the oven and open the door, letting the chicken rest inside for 20 minutes. Serve with rice, naan, lime wedges, and hot lime pickle.

Ingredients

Serves 4

1 chicken, 3 lb 5 oz/1.5 kg

2 tsp garam masala spice mix

1¼ cups plain yogurt

1 onion, finely chopped

2 garlic cloves, crushed

1-inch/2.5-cm piece fresh ginger, peeled and grated

juice of 1 lemon

2 tbsp tomato paste

1 tsp chili powder

1 tsp ground cumin

1 tsp turmeric

1 tbsp paprika (not smoked)

1 tsp salt

to serve

basmati rice

naan

lime wedges

hot lime pickle

BUTTER CHICKEN

Method

Put the onion and the garlic and ginger paste in a food processor, blender, or spice grinder and process until a paste forms. Add the tomatoes, chili powder, sugar, and a pinch of salt and process again until blended.

Melt the ghee in a wok or large skillet over medium–high heat. Add the tomato mixture and water and stir in the tomato paste.

Bring the mixture to a boil, stirring, then reduce the heat to low and simmer for 5 minutes, stirring occasionally, until the sauce thickens.

Stir in half the butter, the garam masala, cumin, and coriander. Add the chicken pieces and stir until they are well coated. Simmer for about an additional 10 minutes, or until the chicken is hot. Taste and adjust the seasoning, if necessary.

Lightly beat the cream in a small bowl and stir in several tablespoons of the hot sauce, beating continuously. Stir the cream mixture into the tomato sauce, then add the remaining butter and stir until it melts. Garnish with the chopped cashew nuts and cilantro sprigs and serve straight from the wok.

Ingredients

Serves 4–6

1 onion, chopped

1½ tbsp garlic and ginger paste

14 oz/400 g canned chopped tomatoes

¼–½ tsp chili powder

pinch of sugar

2 tbsp ghee, vegetable oil, or peanut oil

½ cup water

1 tbsp tomato paste

3 tbsp butter, cut into small pieces

½ tsp garam masala

½ tsp ground cumin

½ tsp ground coriander

8 cooked tandoori chicken pieces

4 tbsp heavy cream

salt and pepper

chopped cashew nuts and fresh cilantro sprigs, to garnish

MUTTON BURRA

Ingredients

Makes 12

12 rib lamb chops, about 1¼ inches/3.5 cm thick, with the meat of each chop sliced several times and the bones scraped

vegetable oil, for greasing

3 tbsp ghee or butter, melted

chopped fresh cilantro

tandoori marinade

1¼ cups plain yogurt, strained through cheesecloth for at least 2 hours, or heaped ¾ cup Greek-style yogurt

2 large garlic cloves, finely chopped

½ tbsp grated fresh ginger

1 tsp ground cinnamon

1 tsp ground cumin

½ tsp ground coriander

½ tsp cayenne pepper, or to taste

pinch ground cloves

pinch ground turmeric

salt and pepper

Method

To make the marinade, put all the ingredients, with some salt and pepper, into a plastic bag large enough to hold all the chops and mix together well. Add the ribs, seal the bag, and let marinate for 4–24 hours.

When ready to cook, line a broiler pan with foil and brush the rack with a little vegetable oil. Remove the chops from the marinade and wipe the ribs clean. Arrange the chops on the rack and drizzle with half the ghee.

Broil the chops for 10 minutes, then turn over and drizzle with the remaining ghee. Continue broiling for an additional 8 minutes for medium or 10 minutes for well done. Let stand for at least 2 minutes, then sprinkle with cilantro and serve. These can be served hot or cold.

MEATBALLS IN CREAMY CASHEW NUT SAUCE

Ingredients

Serves 4

1 lb/450 g fresh lean ground lamb

1 tbsp thick plain yogurt

1 large egg, beaten

½ tsp ground cardamom

½ tsp ground nutmeg

½ tsp pepper

½ tsp dried mint

½ tsp salt, or to taste

1¼ cups cold water

1-inch/2.5-cm piece cinnamon stick

5 green cardamom pods

5 cloves

2 bay leaves

3 tbsp sunflower oil or olive oil

1 onion, finely chopped

2 tsp garlic paste

1 tsp ground ginger

1 tsp ground fennel seeds

½ tsp ground turmeric

½–1 tsp chili powder

generous 1 cup cashew nuts, soaked in ⅔ cup boiling water for 20 minutes

⅔ cup heavy cream

1 tbsp crushed pistachios, to garnish

Method

Put the lamb into a bowl and add the yogurt, egg, cardamom, nutmeg, pepper, mint, and salt. Knead the meat until it is smooth and velvety. Chill for 30–40 minutes, then divide into quarters. Make five balls out of each quarter and roll them between your palms to make them smooth and neat.

Bring the cold water to a boil in a large saucepan and add all the whole spices and the bay leaves. Arrange the meatballs in a single layer, reduce the heat to medium, cover the pan, and cook for 12–15 minutes. Remove the meatballs, cover, and keep hot. Strain the spiced stock and set aside.

Wipe out the pan and add the oil. Place over medium heat and add the onion and garlic paste. Cook until the mixture begins to brown and add the ground ginger, fennel, turmeric, and chili powder. Stir-fry for 2–3 minutes, then add the strained stock and meatballs. Bring to a boil, reduce the heat to low, cover, and simmer for 10–12 minutes.

Meanwhile, process the cashew nuts to a paste in a blender and add to the meatball mixture, along with the cream. Simmer for an additional 5–6 minutes, then remove from the heat. Garnish with crushed pistachios and serve.

ALMOND AND PISTACHIO DESSERT

Ingredients

Serves 6

5½ tbsp unsalted butter

2 cups ground almonds

1 cup sugar

⅔ cup light cream

8 almonds, chopped

10 pistachios, chopped

Method

Melt the butter in a heavy-bottom pan, preferably nonstick, stirring well. Add the ground almonds, sugar, and cream, stirring well. Reduce the heat and stir constantly for 10–12 minutes, scraping the bottom of the pan.

Increase the heat until the mixture turns a little darker in color.

Transfer the almond mixture to a large, shallow serving dish and smooth the top with the back of a spoon.

Decorate the top of the dessert with the chopped almonds and pistachios. Let set for 1 hour, then cut into diamond shapes and serve cold.

SALT LASSI

Ingredients

Serves 4–6

3 cups plain yogurt

½ tsp salt

¼ tsp sugar

generous 1 cup water

ice cubes

ground cumin and fresh mint sprigs,
to decorate

Method

Beat the yogurt, salt, and sugar together in a pitcher or bowl, then add the water and whisk until frothy.

Fill 4–6 glasses with ice cubes and pour over the yogurt mixture. Lightly dust the top of each glass with ground cumin and decorate with mint sprigs.

AAM KI KULFI

Ingredients

Serves 6–8

heaping 1½ cups canned evaporated milk

1¼ cups light cream

¼ cup ground almonds

½–⅓ cup granulated sugar

1 lb/450 g mango puree

1 tsp freshly ground cardamom seeds

scant ¼ cup shelled unsalted pistachios,
to decorate

Method

Pour the evaporated milk and cream into a heavy-bottom saucepan and stir to mix. Put over medium heat. Mix the ground almonds and sugar together, then add to the milk mixture. Cook, stirring, for 6–8 minutes, until the mixture thickens slightly.

Remove from the heat and let the mixture cool completely, stirring from time to time to prevent a skin from forming. When completely cold, stir in the mango puree and ground cardamom.

Meanwhile, preheat a small saucepan over medium heat, add the pistachios, and toast for 2–3 minutes. Let cool, then lightly crush. Store in an airtight container until required.

Kulfi is set in traditional conical-shape plastic or steel molds, which you can buy from Asian stores, but you can use decorative individual molds or ice-pop molds instead. Fill the containers of your choice with the kulfi mixture and freeze for 5–6 hours. Traditional molds hold about 2 tablespoons of the kulfi mixture, but you can use larger containers if you like. Transfer the kulfi to the refrigerator for 40 minutes, then cut into portions with a sharp knife. Serve sprinkled with the crushed pistachios to decorate.

BANGKOK

Clear, clean flavors from coconut, ginger, lime, and tamarind, and blasts of heat from some of the world's hottest chiles sum up the essence of Bangkok's tantalizing food. The best Thai cooking involves complex preparation and has evolved from the royal kitchens, but Bangkok also has an established tradition of street food, prepared to order by vendors for eating on the go. Easy-to-make Green Chicken Curry, for example, now popular around the world, is typical street food. All the dishes of a typical Bangkok meal are served at once. This provides an interesting mix of textures from steamed and crispy stir-fried dishes, soft noodles, and tender rice, and exciting flavor combinations, along with refreshing and crunchy salads. The result is meals that satisfy.

THAI TOM YUM SOUP WITH FISH

Ingredients

Serves 6

5½ cups light chicken stock

6 lemongrass stalks, crushed to release their flavor

3 tbsp very finely chopped cilantro roots

10 kaffir lime leaves, central stalks torn off

1 red chile, seeded and finely chopped

1-inch/2.5-cm piece of galangal (or fresh ginger), peeled and thinly sliced

3 tbsp nam pla

1 tbsp sugar

1 lb 2 oz/500 g shrimp, shelled except for the tails

1 lb 2 oz/500 g firm white fish, such as cod or monkfish, chopped into bite-size pieces

8 oz/225 g canned bamboo shoots or water chestnuts

12 cherry tomatoes, halved

juice of 2 limes

handful of fresh cilantro leaves and handful of fresh basil leaves, chopped, to garnish

Method

Pour the stock into a large saucepan and add the lemongrass, cilantro roots, lime leaves, chile, galangal, nam pla, and sugar. Cover the saucepan. Bring to a boil, then reduce the heat and simmer for 10 minutes.

Add the shrimp, fish, and bamboo shoots and simmer for an additional 4 minutes. Add the tomatoes and lime juice and check the seasoning, adding more fish sauce and sugar, if necessary.

Remove and discard the lemongrass stalks, then divide the soup between six bowls and scatter over the cilantro and basil leaves.

CORN FRITTERS

Ingredients

Serves 4

3 scallions, chopped finely

11½ oz/325 g canned corn kernels, drained

1 red bell pepper, seeded and finely chopped

small handful of fresh cilantro, chopped

2 garlic cloves, crushed

2 eggs

2 tsp superfine sugar

1 tbsp fish sauce

2 tbsp rice flour or cornstarch

vegetable or peanut oil, for pan-frying

dip

2 red bell peppers, seeded and halved

2 tomatoes, peeled, seeded, and chopped coarsely

1 tbsp vegetable or peanut oil, for pan-frying

1 onion, chopped

1 tbsp red curry paste

3–4 sprigs fresh cilantro, chopped

Method

Combine all the ingredients for the fritters in a bowl. Heat the oil in a skillet and cook spoonfuls of the mixture, in batches, until golden brown on the underside. Flip over with a spatula to cook the second side. Remove from the skillet, drain on paper towels, and keep warm.

To make the dip, put the red bell peppers on a baking sheet and place, skin-side up, under a hot broiler, until blackened. Using tongs, transfer to a plastic bag, tie the top, and let cool slightly.

When the bell peppers are cool enough to handle, peel off the skins and chop the flesh. Put into a blender or food processor with the tomatoes and process until smooth.

Heat the oil in a heavy-bottom pan and cook the onion and curry paste for 3–4 minutes, until softened. Add the bell pepper and tomato puree and cook gently until tender and hot. Stir in the chopped cilantro, cook for 1 minute, and serve hot with the fritters.

WONTONS

Ingredients

Serves 4

filling

2 tbsp vegetable or peanut oil

6 scallions, chopped

2 cups chopped mushrooms

2 oz/55 g fine green beans, chopped

¼ cup corn kernels, drained if canned

1 egg, beaten

3 tbsp Thai soy sauce

1 tbsp jaggery or light brown sugar

½ tsp salt

plum or chili sauce, to serve

wontons

24 wonton skins

1 egg, beaten

vegetable or peanut oil, for deep-frying

Method

To make the filling, heat the oil in a preheated wok and stir-fry the scallions, mushrooms, and beans for 1–2 minutes, until softened. Add the corn, stir well to mix, and then push the vegetables to the side. Pour in the egg. Stir until lightly set before incorporating the vegetables and adding the soy sauce, sugar, and salt. Remove the wok from the heat.

Place the wonton skins in a pile on a counter. Put a teaspoonful of the filling in the center of the top skin. Brush the edges with beaten egg and fold in half diagonally to make a small triangular package. Repeat with the remaining skins and filling.

Heat the oil for deep-frying in a wok or large skillet. Add the packages, in batches, and deep-fry for 3–4 minutes, until golden brown. Remove from the wok with a slotted spoon and drain on paper towels. Keep warm while you cook the remaining wontons. Serve hot with plum or chili sauce.

GREEN CHICKEN CURRY

Method

Heat the oil in a wok or large skillet and stir-fry the onion and garlic for 1–2 minutes, until starting to soften. Add the curry paste and stir-fry for 1–2 minutes.

Add the coconut milk, stock, and lime leaves, bring to a boil, and add the chicken. Reduce the heat and let simmer gently for 15–20 minutes, until the chicken is tender.

Add the fish sauce, soy sauce, lime rind and juice, and sugar. Cook for 2–3 minutes, until the sugar has dissolved. Serve immediately, garnished with chopped cilantro.

Ingredients

Serves 4

1 tbsp vegetable or peanut oil

1 onion, sliced

1 garlic clove, chopped finely

2–3 tbsp green curry paste

1¾ cups coconut milk

⅔ cup chicken stock

4 kaffir lime leaves

4 skinless, boneless chicken breasts, cut into cubes

1 tbsp fish sauce

2 tbsp Thai soy sauce

grated rind and juice of ½ lime

1 tsp jaggery or light brown sugar

4 tbsp chopped fresh cilantro, to garnish

MONKFISH AND LIME WITH CHILI SAUCE

Ingredients

Serves 4

four 4-oz/115 g monkfish fillets

¼ cup rice flour or cornstarch

6 tbsp vegetable or peanut oil

4 garlic cloves, crushed

2 large fresh red chiles, seeded and sliced

2 tsp jaggery or light brown sugar

juice of 2 limes

grated rind of 1 lime

boiled rice, to serve

Method

Toss the fish in the flour, shaking off any excess. Heat the oil in a wok and cook the fish on all sides until browned and cooked through, being careful when turning not to break it up.

Lift the fish out of the wok and keep warm. Add the garlic and chiles and stir-fry for 1–2 minutes, until they have softened.

Add the sugar, the lime juice and rind, and 2–3 tablespoons of water and bring to a boil. Let simmer gently for 1–2 minutes, then spoon the mixture over the fish. Serve immediately with rice.

CRISPY PORK DUMPLINGS

Ingredients

Serves 4

1½ cups ground pork

2 tbsp finely chopped fresh cilantro

1 garlic clove, crushed

1 fresh green chile, seeded and chopped

3 tbsp cornstarch

1 egg white

½ tsp salt

16 wonton skins

1 tbsp water

vegetable or peanut oil, for cooking

chili sauce, to serve

Method

Put the pork in a bowl and beat in the cilantro, garlic, chile, 1 tablespoon of the cornstarch, the egg white, and salt. Beat together to a thick, smooth texture. With damp hands, shape into 16 equal portions and roll into balls.

Put a pork ball in the center of each wonton skin. Make a paste by mixing the remaining cornstarch with 1 tablespoon of water. Brush the edges of the skins with the cornstarch paste and gather them up around the filling to make half into small, sacklike packages, and the rest into triangular shapes.

Arrange the dumplings in a single layer (in batches if necessary) in the top of a steamer and cook over boiling water for 10–15 minutes, until the meat is cooked through.

Heat the oil in a wok or large skillet and carefully drop the packages into it. Deep-fry for 2–3 minutes, until golden brown and crisp. Drain on paper towels and serve hot with chili sauce.

SPICY BEEF WITH POTATO

Method

Cut the beef into thick slices and place in a shallow dish. Put the soy sauce, fish sauce, 1 tablespoon of the oil, the cilantro roots, peppercorns, garlic, and sugar in a food processor and process to a thick paste. Scrape the paste into the dish and toss the beef to coat. Cover with plastic wrap and set aside to marinate in the refrigerator for at least 3 hours, preferably overnight.

Heat the remaining oil in a wok. Lift the beef out of the marinade, reserving the marinade, and cook for 3–4 minutes on each side, until browned. Add the reserved marinade and the potatoes with the measured water and gradually bring to a boil. Let simmer for 6–8 minutes, or until the potatoes are tender.

Add the scallions and spinach. Cook gently until the greens have wilted. Serve immediately with rice or noodles.

Ingredients

Serves 4–6

1 lb/450 g beef fillet

2 tbsp Thai soy sauce

2 tbsp fish sauce

2 tbsp vegetable or peanut oil

3–4 cilantro roots, chopped

1 tbsp crushed black peppercorns

2 garlic cloves, chopped

1 tbsp jaggery or light brown sugar

12 oz/350 g potatoes, diced

⅔ cup water

bunch of scallions, chopped

5 cups baby spinach leaves

cooked rice or noodles, to serve

SPICY RICE PUDDING

Ingredients

Serves 6

1¾ cups canned coconut milk

⅔ cup milk

generous ¼ cup light brown sugar

generous ¼ cup short-grain rice

2 tsp allspice

2 tbsp butter

1 tsp ground cinnamon

Method

Put the coconut milk and milk in a pan and heat gently. Add the sugar and stir until it has dissolved.

Add the rice and allspice and gradually bring to a boil. Let simmer gently, stirring frequently, for 45–60 minutes, until thickened.

Stir in the butter, and once it has melted, serve immediately, sprinkled with cinnamon.

PINEAPPLE AND LIME SORBET

Ingredients

Serves 4

generous 1 cup superfine sugar

2½ cups water

grated rind and juice of 2 limes

1 small pineapple, peeled, quartered, and chopped

sweet cookies, to serve

Method

Put the sugar and water into a pan and heat gently, stirring until the sugar has dissolved. Bring to a boil and let simmer for 10 minutes.

Stir in the grated rind and half the lime juice. Remove from the heat and let cool.

Put the pineapple in a blender or food processor and process until smooth. Add to the cold syrup with the remaining lime juice. Pour into a freezerproof container and freeze until crystals have formed around the edge.

Turn out the sherbet into a bowl. Beat well with a fork to break up the crystals. Return to the freezer and chill overnight. Serve in scoops with sweet cookies.

GRILLED BANANAS

Method

Put the creamed coconut and heavy cream in a small saucepan and heat gently until the coconut has dissolved. Remove from the heat and set aside to cool for 10 minutes, then whisk until thick but floppy.

Peel the bananas and coat in the lime juice and rind. Lightly oil a preheated grill pan and cook the bananas, turning once, for 2–3 minutes, until soft and browned.

Toast the dry unsweetened coconut on a piece of foil under a broiler until lightly browned. Serve the bananas with the coconut cream, sprinkled with the toasted coconut.

Ingredients

Serves 4

¼ cup coconut cream or milk

⅓ cup heavy cream

4 bananas

juice and rind of 1 lime

1 tbsp vegetable or peanut oil

⅔ cup unsweetened, dried flaked coconut

Melbourne

Melbourne's food culture offers great variety with a real enjoyment of upmarket, trendy, and simple dining. A food revolution has swept through Australia in the past couple of decades, but the country's second city has steadfastly maintained its reputation as the top food city. The chefs have always been known for their sophisticated style, and their enthusiasm for embracing the ingredients and flavors brought by Asian, Greek, and Middle Eastern immigrants has resulted in what's known as Mod Oz cooking—Lightly Seared Kangaroo on Polenta is an example of this contemporary, fusion-style of food. Grilling never goes out of fashion, and Empire favorites from England, such as Sticky Date Pudding and Apple & Rhubarb Crumble, remain popular with the city's discerning diners.

Salt & Pepper Squid

Ingredients

Serves 4

2 tsp coarse sea salt

½ tsp Szechuan or black peppercorns

14 oz/400 g cleaned squid bodies, tentacles removed and bodies cut into ¼-inch/5-mm rings

about 2 tbsp cornstarch

sunflower oil or peanut oil, for frying

½ tbsp finely chopped fresh parsley (optional)

4 iceberg lettuce or radicchio leaf cups and lemon wedges, to serve

Method

Put the salt in a mortar and grind with a pestle. Add the peppercorns, pound to crush them lightly, and grind until both seasonings are very fine, then set aside. Meanwhile, bring a large saucepan of water to a boil.

Drop the squid rings into the boiling water and cook for 15 seconds. They will form loops and lose their translucent whiteness. Do not overcook. Drain and refresh under cold running water. Shake dry, then tip onto a clean dish towel and pat dry. Put the cornstarch on a plate.

Heat 2 inches/5 cm of the oil in a wok or deep skillet to 350°F/180°C, or until a cube of bread browns in 30 seconds. Coat half the squid rings in the cornstarch and shake off the excess. Drop them in the oil and fry for 20 seconds. Use a slotted spoon to remove them from the oil and drain on folded paper towels. Return the oil to the correct temperature and cook the remaining squid rings.

Sprinkle the hot squid rings with the salt-and-pepper mixture to taste and add parsley for color, if using. Toss to distribute the seasoning, then divide between the lettuce cups. Serve at once with lemon wedges on the side for squeezing over. Any leftover seasoning mixture will keep in an airtight container in a cupboard for several months.

Pear, Arugula & Bleu Cheese Salad with Balsamic Vinaigrette

Method

To make the dressing, put the oil, vinegar, and salt and pepper to taste in a large nonmetallic bowl and whisk until blended and thick. Cover and set aside.

Just before serving, quarter, core, and thinly slice the pear, adding it to the bowl with the dressing as it is prepared, then gently toss so all the pieces are coated with dressing. Add the arugula and cheese and toss again to combine. Sprinkle the pine nuts over and serve.

Ingredients

Serves 4–6

1 pear, such as Bosc

2 bunches wild arugula, rinsed and shaken dry

¾ cup crumbled bleu cheese, such as Gorgonzola

3 tbsp pine nuts, toasted

dressing

4 tbsp extra virgin olive oil

1 tbsp balsamic vinegar

salt and pepper

Bruschetta with Vine-Ripened Tomatoes, Basil & Olive Oil

Ingredients

Makes 8

4 firm vine-ripened plum tomatoes, peeled, cored, seeded, and finely chopped

8 slices ciabatta, about ½ inch/1 cm thick

good fruity olive oil

2 or 3 large garlic cloves, halved

sea salt

basil leaves, to garnish

Method

Put the tomatoes in a nylon strainer over a bowl, sprinkle with salt, and let drain. Meanwhile, heat the broiler to high, with the broiler rack positioned 4 inches/10 cm from the heat.

Brush both sides of all the bread with olive oil. Place on the rack and broil for 2 minutes, or until crisp and lightly browned, then turn and broil on the other side. Remove the toast from the heat and rub one side of each with the garlic, pressing down firmly.

Shake the strainer to remove any moisture from the tomatoes, then divide them between the toasts. Drizzle with a little more olive oil and scatter basil leaves over, then serve.

Lightly Seared Kangaroo on Polenta

Method

Preheat the oven to 225°F/110°C. Bring 3 cups of water to a boil in a large saucepan. Melt 1 tablespoon of the butter with the oil in a large skillet over medium heat. Add the onions and fry, stirring occasionally, for 3 minutes. Add the garlic and continue stirring for 2 minutes, or until the onions are softened and browned. Use a slotted spoon to remove the onions from the skillet and keep warm in the preheated oven.

Add a little oil to the skillet, if necessary. Season the steaks with salt and pepper on both sides, then add to the skillet over medium–high heat and fry for 3 minutes. Turn the steaks over and fry for an additional 3 minutes for medium or 4–5 minutes for well done. Remove from the skillet, add to the onions, and keep warm.

Add the wine and rosemary to the skillet and bring to a boil, scraping the skillet with a wooden spoon. Season with salt and pepper and let bubble until reduced to about half.

Meanwhile, add the polenta and ½ teaspoon salt to the boiling water in a steady stream, stirring, and boil for 1 minute, or according to the package directions, until thickened and softened. Add salt and pepper to taste.

Pour any juices from the onions and kangaroo into the bubbling wine and adjust the seasoning, if necessary. Transfer the steaks to warmed plates, strain the wine into a small pitcher, and pour over, then add a mound of polenta.

Ingredients

Serves 4

6 tbsp butter

2 tbsp olive oil, plus extra, if needed for frying

2 large onions, thinly sliced

2 garlic cloves, crushed

4 kangaroo fillet steaks, about 4½ oz/125 g each and 1 in/2.5 cm thick

1¼ cups dry red wine, such as Shiraz

sprig of fresh rosemary

1¼ cups quick-cook polenta

salt and pepper

Seared Tuna with Green Olive Dressing

Method

Up to a day before cooking, put all the ingredients for the dressing in a nonmetallic bowl, adding the chile, if using, with salt and pepper to taste, then cover and set aside until required.

When ready to cook, heat a large, dry cast-iron ridged grill pan over very high heat until a splash of water "dances" on the surface. Brush one surface of each steak with oil from the dressing, then place oiled-side down on the pan and cook for 2 minutes.

Brush the top of the steaks with more oil from the dressing, then, using tongs, flip the steaks over, season to taste with salt and pepper, and continue cooking for an additional 30 seconds for rare or up to 2 minutes for well done.

Transfer the steaks to plates and spoon a little of the dressing over each. Serve the remaining dressing separately, along with plenty of bread to mop up the rich oil.

Ingredients

Serves 4

4 tuna steaks, about 5½ oz/150 g each and ½ inch/1 cm thick

sea salt and pepper

crusty bread, to serve

dressing

1 cup garlic-flavored olive oil

1 generous cup chopped meaty pitted green olives

4 anchovy fillets in olive oil, chopped

4 tbsp fresh orange juice

finely grated zest of 1 large orange

½ tsp ground cumin

¼ tsp ground coriander

squeeze of lemon juice

1 fresh red chile, seeded and finely chopped, or to taste (optional)

salt and pepper

Barbecued-Asian-Flavored Poussins

Method

To make the marinade, mix all the ingredients together in a nonmetallic bowl large enough to hold both poussins, then set aside.

Ease the skin from the breast flesh on both birds. Gently slide the orange slices under the skin, then ease the skin back over the slices. Put the poussins in the marinade and rub the mixture all over. Cover with plastic wrap and let marinate in the refrigerator for 4–24 hours, turning occasionally.

Remove the poussins from the refrigerator 20 minutes in advance of cooking. Heat the grill. Brush the rack with olive oil and position it about 4 inches/10 cm above the heat. Spear each poussin with two long metal skewers, from left to right at the top and bottom, to keep them flat. Put the birds on the grill rack, breast-side down, and grill for 20–25 minutes on each side, basting occasionally with the remaining marinade, until the juices run clear when the thighs are pierced.

Let rest for 10 minutes, then cut each bird in half and remove the orange slices. Alternatively, preheat the oven to 350°F/180°C. Heat a large, ridged cast-iron grill pan over high heat until a splash of water "dances" on the surface. Brush with olive oil, then add the unskewered birds and cook 10 minutes, or until brown. Turn the birds over and put the pan in the preheated oven for an additional 30 minutes, basting occasionally with the remaining marinade, until the juices run clear when the thighs are pierced.

Meanwhile, mix the olive oil, orange juice, and sesame oil with salt and pepper to taste in a nonmetallic bowl. Add the watercress, bell pepper, and sesame seeds and toss together.

Arrange a portion of salad on each plate and serve with half a poussin on top. Sprinkle with cilantro and serve hot or at room temperature.

Ingredients

Serves 4

2 poussins, about 1 lb/450 g each, butterflied

1 orange, thinly sliced

4 tbsp extra virgin olive oil, plus extra for oiling

1½ tbsp fresh orange juice

1 tsp sesame oil

14 oz/400 g fresh watercress leaves, trimmed, rinsed, and thoroughly dried

1 red bell pepper, cored, seeded, and thinly shredded with a vegetable peeler

2 tbsp sesame seeds, toasted

salt and pepper

chopped fresh cilantro, to garnish

marinade

6 tbsp sunflower oil

4 tbsp soy sauce

2 tbsp sesame oil

2 garlic cloves, minced

¼-inch/5-mm piece fresh ginger, grated

pinch chile flakes, to taste

Marinated Rack of Lamb with Warm Tomato, Bean & Herb Salad

Ingredients

Serves 3–4

2 racks of lamb with 6 ribs each, chine bones removed

salt and pepper

marinade

4 garlic cloves, crushed

4 tbsp extra virgin olive oil

4 tbsp white wine vinegar

1 tbsp smooth mustard, such as Dijon

1 tbsp honey

1 tsp fresh oregano leaves

1 tsp fresh thyme leaves

salad

4 tbsp olive oil

2 large tomatoes, halved, cored, and coarsely chopped

2 large garlic cloves, finely chopped

14 oz/400 g canned cannellini beans or butter beans, drained and rinsed

4 scallions, trimmed and finely chopped

1 large peeled red bell pepper in oil, drained and sliced

2 tbsp chopped fresh parsley

2 tbsp chopped fresh mint

squeeze of lemon juice (optional)

salt and pepper

fresh basil leaves, to garnish

Method

To make the marinade, put all the ingredients in a plastic bag. Hold closed and shake to blend the ingredients. Add the racks of lamb, reseal, and shake again. Let marinate in the refrigerator 4–24 hours, shaking occasionally. Remove from the refrigerator 20 minutes before cooking. Preheat the oven to 400°F/200°C.

When ready to cook, remove the meat from the marinade, scrape off the herbs, and pat dry. Place in a roasting pan and sprinkle the fatty surface with salt and pepper. Put the pan in the preheated oven and roast for 25 minutes per 1 lb 2 oz/500 g plus 15 minutes for medium, or 30 minutes per 1 lb 2 oz/500 g plus 15 minutes for well done. Remove from the oven and let rest for 10 minutes before cutting into individual chops.

Meanwhile, to make the salad, heat the oil in a large skillet over medium heat. Add the tomatoes and garlic and stir for 3 minutes, or until the tomatoes soften and start to break down. Stir in the beans, scallions, bell pepper, parsley, mint, and salt and pepper to taste. Stir until all the ingredients are warmed through, then remove from the heat. Add a squeeze of lemon juice, if using, and adjust the seasoning.

Arrange the chops on plates with the warm salad spooned over. Scatter the salad with basil leaves just before serving.

Rhubarb & Apple Crumble

Ingredients

Serves 4–6

1 lb/450 g rhubarb, cut into 1-inch/2.5-cm pieces

3 large apples, such as Granny Smiths, peeled, cored, and chopped

2 tbsp orange juice or apple juice

4 tbsp light brown sugar

4 tbsp butter, cut into pieces

1½-inch/4-cm piece fresh ginger

pouring cream, to serve

topping

1¼ cups all-purpose flour

6 tbsp very cold butter, cut into pieces

scant ½ cup sugar

2 tbsp rolled oats

Method

Heat the oven to 375ºF/190ºC and lightly grease a 5-cup baking dish that is suitable for serving from.

Put the rhubarb, apples, orange juice, and sugar in the dish and mix together. Dot with butter and grate the ginger over.

To make the topping, put the flour in a large bowl and rub in the butter until the mixture forms large crumbs. Stir in the sugar and oats. Sprinkle the mixture over the filling, taking it right up to the edge of the dish.

Place the dish on a baking sheet and bake in the preheated oven for 25–30 minutes until the topping is light brown, the filling is bubbling, and the rhubarb and apples are tender when pierced with a fork. Let stand for 2 minutes, then serve with cream for pouring over.

Maple-Cream Tart

Ingredients

Makes 10–12 slices

13 oz/375 g store-bought flaky pie dough, thawed if frozen

6 tbsp all-purpose flour, plus extra for rolling the dough

3 tbsp light brown sugar

3 cups plus 2 tbsp heavy cream

¾ cup pure maple syrup

2 eggs

4 tsp lemon juice

¾ tsp salt

¼ tsp ground nutmeg

2 tbsp confectioners' sugar

Method

Preheat the oven to 400°F/200°C. Roll out the dough on a lightly floured surface and use to line a 9-inch/23-cm loose-bottom tart pan. Line the dough with wax paper and weigh down with dried beans. Place on a baking sheet and bake in the preheated oven for 15–20 minutes, until golden at the edges.

Meanwhile, combine the flour and sugar in a large bowl. Beat 2 cups of the cream in another bowl with the maple syrup, eggs, lemon juice, salt, and nutmeg. Slowly whisk this mixture into the flour, whisking until no lumps remain.

When the pastry shell is golden, remove the paper and beans and reduce the oven temperature to 350°F/180°C. Pour the filling into the pastry shell, return to the oven, and bake for 30–35 minutes, until set. Remove the tart from the oven and let cool completely on a wire rack.

Whip the remaining cream until soft peaks form. Sift over the confectioners' sugar and continue whipping until stiff. Just before serving, spread the whipped cream over the surface of the tart. Cut into slices to serve.

Sticky Date Puddings

Method

Preheat the oven to 350°F/180°C. Grease four ¾-cup ovenproof bowls or ramekins and dust with flour. Line the bottoms with wax paper.

Beat the butter and sugar until creamed and light. Beat in the eggs, one at a time. Stir in the vanilla extract. Sift over the flour and baking powder and beat in. Slowly add the milk until the batter has a soft dropping consistency; you might not need it all. Fold in the dates. Spoon the mixture into the molds, filling them three-quarters full.

Place the molds in a roasting pan and pour in enough boiling water to come halfway up the sides. Bake in the preheated oven for 40–45 minutes until set and a skewer inserted in the middle of the puddings comes out clean. Remove the molds from the pan and let stand for 2 minutes before turning out onto individual plates.

Meanwhile, to make the sauce, put all the ingredients in a saucepan over medium–high heat, stirring until the sugar melts. Bring to a boil and boil for 5 minutes. Stir in the nuts. Spoon the hot sauce over the puddings and serve at once, with a scoop of ice cream on the side.

Ingredients

Serves 4

6 tbsp butter, softened, plus extra for greasing

scant ½ cup dark brown sugar

3 eggs

½ tsp vanilla extract

⅔ cup self-rising flour, plus extra for dusting

¼ tsp baking powder

about 2 tbsp milk

⅔ cup coarsely chopped, pitted dates, tossed with 1 tbsp all-purpose flour

good-quality vanilla ice cream, to serve

caramel pecan sauce

5 tbsp heavy cream

3 tbsp dark brown sugar

3 tbsp light brown sugar

¾ tsp vanilla extract

4 tbsp chopped pecan nuts

Index